# Grace in
# Ungracious Places

# Grace in Ungracious Places

PRESTON GILLHAM

Fleming H. Revell
A Division of Baker Book House Co
Grand Rapids, Michigan 49516

Published by Fleming H. Revell
a division of Baker Book House Company
P.O. Box 6287, Grand Rapids, MI 49516-6287

Printed in the United States of America

**Library of Congress Cataloging-in-Publication Data**

Gillham, Preston H.
    Grace in ungracious places / Preston Gillham.
        p.     cm.
    ISBN 0-8007-5808-0 (pbk.)
    1. Grace (Theology)  I. Title.
BT761.3 .G55  2002
234—dc21                                                    2002002317

Unless otherwise indicated, Scripture is taken from the NEW AMERICAN STANDARD BIBLE ®, Copyright © The Lockman Foundation 1960, 1962, 1963, 1968, 1971, 1972, 1973, 1975, 1977, 1995. Used by permission.

Scripture marked MESSAGE is taken from THE MESSAGE. Copyright © by Eugene H. Peterson 1993, 1994, 1995. Used by permission of NavPress Publishing Group.

Scripture marked TLB is taken from *The Living Bible* © 1971. Used by permission of Tyndale House Publishers, Inc., Wheaton, IL 60189. All rights reserved.

For current information about all releases from Baker Book House, visit our web site:
http://www.bakerbooks.com

To my sweetheart, Dianne.

Thanks for loving me in—and in spite of—my ungracious places. I have asked Father that I may be so gracious.

I love you, Babe.

# Contents

## Grace in Dangerous Places

## Grace in Ugly Places

## Grace in Insecure Places

# Introduction

For most of my life I have lived in pursuit of a concept—a godly ideal—called grace, considering my quest noble and my goal spiritual. It simply never occurred to me that grace was a person and that he was pursuing me. The grace I sought was small, even though defined in the expanse of biblical terms. It was inhuman, even though associated with Jesus. The grace I envisioned was largely defined by my own theories and guided by the tight parameters I constructed in order to be able to say, "I live according to grace."

It isn't possible for me to put an x on the calendar and say, "There. Right there is where God began to redefine grace for me." As you will see, it has taken a divine effort to break through my human effort to understand grace, and that divine effort has spanned the reaches of my human experience. From the sparrows on my windowsill, to the lounge above a bar in Belize, to the men's room in

Tower One of my office complex, to the Trinity River Trail where I ride my bicycle, God has continued to invade my world. Since his advent at Bethlehem, he has made a repeated and determined effort to share his heart with me.

It is precisely that determined effort, on a variety of fronts, that finally got my attention and emboldened me to abandon what I knew of grace for what he wanted to show me of grace. I worked for years, praying all the while, to craft a better definition of grace. But God surprised me. Instead of answering my prayer and assisting me with a definition of grace, he demonstrated it to me. In his brilliance, he illustrated the magnitude of who he is in the simplicity and darkness of my elementary world.

In a shrewd act of genius, our heavenly Father reveals his grace in ungracious places, just as an astute jeweler displays a diamond against a dark backdrop. People relate to people, and Father wants to make sure we get the point: Grace is a person, and he is engaged in our daily life no matter where that engagement takes him, even dark and ungracious places.

What an incredible journey we are on as we watch God reveal his heart to us. If you have ever had to travel alone, you know the loneliness of a solitary journey. God is no different: He hates to travel by himself. As a matter of fact, he determined that he would rather die than embark on the journey without us. He made the trip from heaven to earth alone and does not intend to return without company. Grace is his invitation to us to reach our destination with him and celebrate the journey throughout eternity.

As you will discover, I have attempted to take you with me on the journey of these pages. Oftentimes, a key thought or the right question is just the thing to keep us moving down the road together. Each chapter offers you "Something to Consider." I challenge you to consider what is there. Ask Father—that is how I refer to God throughout these pages, not because I'm comfortable doing so, but because I wish to honor his request—to guide your thoughts with his own. Ask him to weave another stitch in the tapestry of your life as you consider the central thought of the chapter before you.

In an effort to let you see a little deeper inside my journey and encourage you on yours, I have concluded every chapter with a prayer. Use it as a springboard. Let it focus your thoughts and prepare your heart for the next chapter. In the safety of these pages, listen to see if the song of your heart resonates with my prayer. And don't be put off with the final line of each prayer, "Thanks, Papa." "Papa" is the closest translation the English language has for the term our Older Brother gave to Father, "Abba." "Dad" is close, as are "Pa" and "Daddy." The amazing thing is that God will answer to any of these names.

I hope and pray that the honesty of my journey will be of benefit to you. We are in this life together. While some of my struggles will not be your struggles, God's determination to share his heart with us in spite of the ungraciousness of life is the common denominator we share. From the highest high, to the lowest low, to the boring apathy of the middle places, there is no place too high, too low, or too mundane to alter Father's steady revelation of his heart.

May the profound realization of grace in your ungracious places inspire you to say, "Oh, wow!" And with that, I pray you will pledge to allow his perspective of grace to change the *what* you know of grace to the *who* you know that is grace.

God bless you, my friend.

# Grace in

# Ordinary
# Places

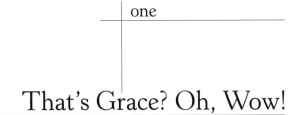

# one

# That's Grace? Oh, Wow!

Grace. It is a woman's name. It is what I hope for from the police officer who clocked me doing forty-four in a thirty-five. It is a theological concept. It is the acrostic **G**od's **R**iches **A**t **C**hrist's **E**xpense. It is a silver bullet neutralizing hell and granting heaven's reprieve. It is synonymous with the compassion of God preventing him from exacting justice on a deserving group of hellions. It is an ideal of little value to the concerns hounding me Monday through Saturday. It is an irrelevant subpoint in the pastor's sermon on Sunday morning as I grapple with guilt on Sunday afternoon.

Are grace and un-grace, graciousness and ungraciousness, mutually exclusive? Is there some pivotal point where life teeters between the two? Do I live in either grace or un-grace, manifest either graciousness or ungraciousness?

15

Does grace parade itself on the Spirit-filled side of life and call to me in my ungraciousness to extract myself from the mire of my many messes and join in the pursuit of God? I don't think so. On the contrary.

While I have lived much of my life by these notions, now that I am older, I have come to grips more graphically with the failure of my fleshly efforts. I have just enough wisdom to recognize the bankrupt abilities of my giftedness to win acceptance with God and see a different grace than the one of my younger days. Instead of a concept, I see a person. Instead of a theological tenet, I see a sacrifice. Instead of an abstract sermon, I see a life laid down. Instead of a distant goal, I see the strong arm of my heavenly Father. Instead of a lofty ideal, I see an incarnate God. Instead of a golden rule, I see an engaged God desperately attempting what only he would try: an invasion of hell to bring the heaven of his heart to my wounded concept of who he is.

Grace is the good news that God is not aloof. Grace is the encouraging declaration that he is present and engaged. Grace is God's pursuit to encounter me face-to-face. Grace is a royal robe carelessly cast off across the arm of heaven's throne to don the humility and certain demise of humanity. Grace is the invasion of all that God is into all that he is not in the world where I live. Grace is the passionate determination of God to share his heart with me.

Why? In hopes that I will notice and recognize his overture. In hopes that I will see him in all that concerns me and, in so doing, invite his participation in all that I encounter. In hopes that I will find in him a new life rooted in his demonstration of grace—Jesus Christ. In hopes that I will discover his great gift to me of a new heart capable of bonding with his heart of grace. In hopes that he will find in me a partner to journey through life with and share eternity with.

So great is Father's desire to share his heart of grace with us that he is determined to reveal his grace even in ungracious places. So vast is his passion for this overarching mission that he almost seems to sacrifice his character of justice, holiness, and righteousness to enter the barrooms, brawls, and backstreets of my ungraciousness and meet me at my point of discovery. So unfathomable is his determination to reveal his grace that it is beyond the constitution and bylaws of the church, the staid and moralistic standards of many saints, and the exhortation of many of our revered and religious elders. But so profound is his grace that it will tolerate the ungraciousness of the world under our fingernails and the stench of un-grace in the fabric of our lives to convey his heart.

Grace in ungracious places is about a God who is not content to sit on his throne while we wallow in the un-grace of the world. Grace in ungracious places is about the heavenly Father intent on sharing his life with his children, in all of our errors of immaturity, in order to celebrate the bond of family heritage throughout all of time and eternity. Grace is about our Father who is determined to run the race, and finish the course, and live inside of us in order to have the satisfaction of saying at the finish line of life, "We did it! Well done! What a great experience we have on which to build our eternal friendship."

Grace is about our heavenly Father who is not afraid to get his hands dirty to be with us as we shovel our way out of life's ungracious messes. Grace is about a divine heart discontent to be by itself. Grace is God's determined effort to share his heart with us in hopes that we will see and recognize and acknowledge his overture and say, "Oh, wow!"

## Something to Consider

Are you open to redefining your definition of grace?

Is it possible you need to risk letting God establish his own parameters of grace?

17

If God were to really be engaged in your life, what would his involvement look like? What would his facial expression be as he conversed with you in the place where you live?

Would God be caught frequenting the places where you live, or is your un-grace too great for his grace?

I have defined grace as God's determined effort to share his heart with you, and I have entitled this book *Grace in Ungracious Places*. My definition of grace and the title of this book are synonymous phrases, and furthermore, they are embodied in a person, and you are related to him. His name is Jesus Christ, and that is a sweet sound.

When God examined his great inventory of options in entering our world, he chose grace, embodied in the baby laid in Bethlehem's manger. He realized his omniscience would be intimidating, his omnipotence debilitating, and his omnipresence disconcerting to us. He knew his love would be disarming. He knew his light would be unapproachable and his justice disabling. So he chose grace and humbled himself to take on human form.

He appeared first in the helplessness of a newborn, the destitution of poverty, the ignominy of a manger, the dishonor of a stable, the shame of illegitimacy, to the recognition of robbers and the derision of the king, with the reputation of being a divisive element, and the object of hatred by the great dragon, Satan. I doubt that there has ever been a more ungracious moment for grace to find itself. But this destitution is the stage God chose for the advent of grace.

Grace in heaven? Yes.

Grace in the church? Yes.

Grace in the world? Certainly.

Grace in the ungracious places of my life and yours? Absolutely. For "where sin increased, grace abounded all the more" (Rom. 5:20).

How is this so? Because grace is a person. Grace is God's heart revealed. Grace is God's effort to become approachable. Grace is God's hope that we will respond.

# MEDITATION
## & RESPONSE

*Father, your grace is amazing, and the sound of these words is sweet.*

*But while these sounds are sweet and I desperately want your grace in my life, I cannot comprehend what I perceive to be the extravagant waste of your heart just to get my attention. I suppose the only chance I have of comprehending the magnitude of your grace is to grasp it each day and examine it within the confines of my ungracious places.*

*Father, thank you for extending your grace to me rather than requiring me to rise to the level of grace. Thank you for giving me your grace as a gift instead of asking me to earn it. Thank you for giving me grace to live as opposed to asking me to live up to its standard.*

*I need your grace, but I need it as it is, not as I have conceived it to be. I need your grace, even though the place I will keep it is rancorous with un-grace. Father, I need your grace to be with me where I live so that I can appreciate who you are and who I am.*

*Father, I need your grace in my ungracious places.*

*Thanks, Papa.*

| two

# The Road to Tomorrow

We consider difficulties, trials, hurts, and challenges as ungracious because they seem so far from what we envision as indicative of God's grace. But I wonder which is correct: Are the unpleasant experiences in life ungracious, or do we have a misunderstanding of God's grace?

As you might know, Scripture is replete with verses detailing the gracious attributes of God. However, there are six biblical authors who discuss Father more lucidly and with greater volume than all of the others. From the heights and depths of their lives, Moses, Samuel, Job, David, John, and Paul make a concerted effort to tell us about him and the intervention of his unfathomable, relentless grace.

Our lives are threaded with the same tapestry of detail as theirs—beautiful from the front but, from the back, knotted and ungracious. The travelogue of their testimony can provide us with a catalyst for growth and encouragement in grace.

Just as the lives of these authors were filled with ungracious circumstances, the same awaits us on the road to tomorrow. But as only mentors can, they offer words of encouragement concerning their journeys and the encompassing grace of God.

In many ways, when Moses wrote Deuteronomy, he was addressing for the last time the people he had given his life to and led to the cusp of the Promised Land. As they stood facing the realization of God's promise, they recognized the prospect of war, temptation, and a new way of life—all under the unproven leadership of Joshua.

What do you suppose Moses spoke of in his final address? He reminded the people of who God is and how the entirety of all that he is preceded them as they contemplated crossing the Jordan River. At the threshold of ungracious uncertainty, Moses encouraged the Israelites to reflect on their foundation.

*The road before us is like a threshold.*

Many years later, during one of the darkest periods of Israel's sordid history, Samuel appeared, calling for revival. He presided as the foremost spiritual and political advisor during the reigns of Saul and David, both of whom he had the privilege of anointing as king. From his earliest days in the temple with Eli, and throughout his life, he referenced who God is.

Samuel was relentless. He continued to listen until he could distinguish between Eli's voice and the voice of God. When searching for the next king of Israel, he continued asking Jesse if he had introduced him to all of his sons until he finally met David, the youngest and most unlikely to be God's chosen servant. He continued to hold Saul accountable, and he was relentless in his obedience to God's command, even to the point of slaying Agag, king of the Amalekites, and hewing him to pieces when Saul would not (see 1 Sam. 15:1–33).

And what did Samuel record in his book? No matter how hard the course or how threatening the circumstances, a relentless determination to see God's perspective always renders the same conclusion: God is faithful!

*The road before us calls for relentless, determined obedience.*

There are few books of the Bible that are more intense and troubling than the Book of Job. From the arrogance of self-justification to the horrific realization of self-righteousness, ungraciousness oozes from nearly every verse. Job demands to know, with cryptic angst, in the midst of immeasurable suffering, why a righteous man like himself suffers like a heathen, only to realize the failure of his own self-sufficiency. Job fills his early chapters with heady, cerebral declarations of who God is, but he concludes his book with heartrending humility as he comes to see the arrogance of his ways and discovers who God truly is.

Job is overwhelmed as he witnesses God's divine character stoop in grace to love him in the rancid fetor of his self-righteousness. It doesn't get worse—or more glorious—than the Book of Job.

*The road to tomorrow is paved with suffering and accompanied by the stench of the flesh.*

Love. Murder. Passion. Grief. Adultery. War. Wealth. Power. David experienced all of these, and more. In fact, the Psalms are his journal, penned from the scope of his emotion and experience. We are privileged to listen in and to let his eloquence speak for us in our moments of grace and un-grace. In so doing, we glimpse the relationship God has in mind when he thinks of us.

*The road to tomorrow is difficult and dangerous.*

Jesus called John "son of thunder." Perhaps most telling, however, is that John refers to himself as the one "whom Jesus loved." He leaned against Jesus during the final supper they shared together. He was one of three men Jesus asked to accompany him during his greatest trial in Gethsemane and his greatest earthly glory on the Mount of Transfiguration. He understood better than any other that Jesus was God incarnate. He stood alone at the cross—contemplate that simple, overlooked fact for a moment—wondering how God could die but remaining faithful to the end.

John expressed the heart of Christianity when he wrote his books. He gave us passionate descriptions of Jesus and a perspective on his life not captured by the other Gospel writers. In simple terms, his books give us many of the great sound bites of our faith: "I go to prepare a place for you"; "In My Father's house are many dwelling places"; "I am the true vine"; "I am the way"; "For God so loved the world"; "I am writing to you, little children, because your sins are forgiven." For these things we are deeply indebted to John, but it is in the way he lived his life and how he thought of himself that he gives us a compelling expression of grace.

*The road to tomorrow has many lonely stretches.*

Paul, the man entrusted more than any other biblical writer to relay to us the truth and systematic theology of God and faith, calls himself the foremost of sinners, the one untimely chosen, the least, a killer, a Pharisee. Well acquainted with his own flesh and temptation, trusted to endure physical burdens that plunged him into the pit of despair and the darkness of death, he was beaten, despondent, disappointed, imprisoned, and misunderstood. But Paul was a man deeply touched by the grace of God. He lived a normal Christian life and sacrificed his life, health, reputation, and profession to tell us about it and inspire us toward the same realization of grace.

Paul was, throughout his life as a believer, a man profoundly humbled by the fact that God chose him to be one of his own. He filled his letters with reminders of who God is, who he made us to be as his children, and who our resource for living must be. According to Paul's inspired words, we are equipped for the road before us.

*The road to tomorrow has a hope and destination pledged by grace.*

As we stand at the threshold of the road before us, we know our lives foreshadow a taste of all that these who have gone before us experienced—grace in ungracious places. But the road to tomorrow is not only a harbinger of circumstantial challenges and emotional upheavals; it also portends glorious revelations of the integrity and character of Father affirmed by the torchbearers of our faith and, I hope, by the testimony of our journey.

Whatever ungraciousness is around the corner of today, Father has traveled the road to tomorrow, and he holds both today and tomorrow graciously in his hand.

## Something to Consider

It is interesting that we are told very little of our future except that "Jesus Christ is the same yesterday and today and forever" (Heb. 13:8). On the other hand, we are told a great deal about today. The passage that first comes to mind is, "Therefore as you have received Christ Jesus the Lord, so walk in Him" (Col. 2:6). Or to paraphrase, "Just as you trusted Christ to save you, trust him, too, for each day's problems" (TLB).

We trust Father by faith, and we are saved by his grace (Eph. 2:8). This is a simple yet monumental remedy. Faith: confidence in God and his ability. Grace: God's determination to share his heart with us. We travel the road to tomorrow with confidence in Father and his resolute determination to travel with us, in us, and through us.

"Do not be worried about your life. . . . Do not worry about tomorrow" (Matt. 6:25a, 34a). When I consider Christ's counsel in light of the road to tomorrow, I cannot picture a well-paved thoroughfare. If the road were smooth and straight, why wouldn't I look into the future? No. I think the road to tomorrow demands my constant attention for each footstep. If I become engrossed in tomorrow, I will stub my toe, bust my nose, or, worse yet, run my life into the ditch today.

Why should I be intent on today? Today is this moment—the current one—where Father is most real to me. It is the only moment I am guaranteed and, therefore, is the moment of my greatest need. Today means facing the demons of right now where I am most tempted to live independently. It is only in the overwhelming largeness of this moment that I can fathom the immensity of God's story instead of projecting my small scope of the future onto today in hopes of managing it myself. Today holds me accountable for trusting Father's grace rather than contemplating the ingenuity I might foist upon tomorrow.

What is before you now?

What is Father's word for you today?

What is your connection to his grace in this very moment?

## MEDITATION & RESPONSE

> *Father, as I contemplate the road to tomorrow, I realize I face only today. While I know you say, "My grace is sufficient," and I assume that means for tomorrow, I realize you*

*take care of tomorrow by providing your grace today.*

*I know—boy, do I know—that this life is filled with ungraciousness. Father, as I consider life, I ask that you grant me the discernment and wisdom to see your grace in ungracious places.*

*Thanks, Papa.*

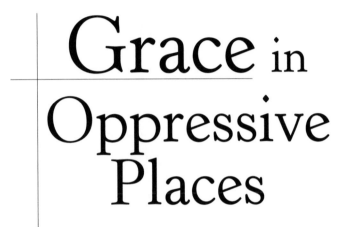

# Grace in
# Oppressive
# Places

# three

# Stalked by the Big Cat

I've just returned from my walk with Honey—Honey Bunch Gillham, our "used dog." We picked Honey up from a rescue group several years ago, and she is now a full-fledged member of the family. She's a Basenji, the barkless breed from Egypt—best friend to the pharaohs— with red and white hair, pricked ears, chiseled face, wrinkled forehead, and curled tail. She weighs in at twenty-five pounds and was bred to hunt lions on the plains of Africa. She's a great companion, but man, is she hardheaded! Once you get her pointed in the right direction, it's a wonderful thing. But accomplishing that goal takes a firm hand and a stronger will than Honey's.

Enter yours truly. Much like Honey, I can be determined, which is a wonderful thing most of the time. However, the enemy has been attempting to use my determination to his advantage. This isn't anything unusual. In fact, it's predictable. Unguarded strengths are a favorite target of the devil. To unwary believers functioning from individual strengths, the last thing to cross their minds is that they are vulnerable to attack.

For example, what did Peter claim just prior to his denial of Christ? That he would follow him to the death. History is replete with examples of armies that held the advantageous position but didn't guard their strengths and suffered defeat. Remember the British occupation of Boston during the Revolutionary War? They lost the city to Washington and the Continental army, and not a shot was fired.

While there isn't anything uncommon about the enemy of God attacking our strengths, it is still disconcerting. Satan prowls about as a lion on the hunt, stalking, watching, seeking someone to devour. He will do whatever it takes to undermine the power of God, and attacking strengths and their corresponding weaknesses is a vintage tactic of deception for him.

To date, the greatest ongoing issue in my spiritual life is distrusting God. I know it is God's will for me to trust him—versus the confidence I have in myself—and I'm determined to do so, but it is this point of attack where I have sustained the greatest losses in the battle. It is here I have been pounced on more times than I can count.

While Honey and I were out walking, the enemy stalked me with accusations concerning God's trustworthiness. What the perceived slight was that I attributed to God, I don't recall. The devil doesn't need much of an opportunity to launch an all-out, full-scale attack.

Like any genuine temptation, the devil's accusations made perfect sense emotionally, experientially, and rationally. The weight of Satan's rationale is so overwhelming it renders spiritual analysis inept and the voice of the Spirit almost inaudible. It will take time for me to realize the disconnect between the devil's reasoning and the counsel of God's Word. Giving me the dignity of choice, the Holy Spirit whispers his grace to me rather than bowling me over with the power of his divine perspective.

The battle over God's character and reputation ensued down Hastings, across Wedgworth Road, and around the cul-de-sac on Whitman Place. It was as though I was a trapped mouse being batted back and forth between the lion's merciless paws.

Thoughts seeped into my mind: *Is God dropping the ball and being unreasonable as the devil asserts? Is God compromising my well-being? Is he taking advantage of me? Don't I have a right to know? After all, it is my life. Why do I always suffer the hard lessons, the bump and grind of life, instead of realizing some of the glorious miracles those folks on TV always talk about?*

Somewhere along about the fireplug and the hedge where the white cat hangs out, voicing my wounds and feeling shame, I said out loud, "Lord God! What the devil says is true. I don't understand what you are doing. I don't have all the information I need."

And I walked on, mostly in silence. I was aware that I had lost valuable territory on the battlefield. I felt disgust and shame for whining and complaining. I felt weak that I had not been strong like a believer ought to be. Condemnation, my familiar nemesis, appeared at my face, his stale breath insulting my worthiness to breathe God's air. Not only did I feel the shame of being disloyal to God by questioning his plan, but I also felt jumped on, slighted, and as though I was God's least favorite child.

And in that ungracious moment, in the clutches of the devil's claws, I began to reason from the perspective of grace and God's Word. Muttering to myself, "I am not condemned (Rom. 8:1), and I don't have to understand. I don't have to have all the information in my hands. I would just pretend I was God if I understood everything he was doing. That's a bad plan. If I could see his hand I wouldn't have the opportunity to trust his heart."

It was as though the steady tug of the Holy Spirit slowly turned the bow of my perspective toward the harbor of God's grace and urged me gently into position where I could drop anchor in the deep waters of his compassion, understanding, and respite.

"Satan! You are attempting to deceive me," I said aloud. My spiritual eyes began to adjust to the darkness of the devil's strategy, and his accusations of shame, disgust, and condemnation were replaced with godly indignation.

"Get away from me, Satan! I will not live in the hell you paint with enticing colors in exchange for the glory of Father's grace.

"Father, you have everything under control, and I choose to trust you. In all honesty, Papa, if I were God I wouldn't do things the way you are doing them. I suppose that is an obvious vulnerability given the temptation that has just flanked me. But, I'm very aware of the fact that there is one God, and I'm not him. You are. You don't have to explain yourself to me as the enemy is implying. For the record—yours, mine, and the devil's—I trust you, Father. Period. End of debate."

In my experience, trust and faith have been used synonymously, yet each has a unique flavor. Satan has taken advantage of this lack of distinction to trip me up. Faith says, "I believe." Trust says, "I believe in spite of the circumstances." Faith requires a willful decision and set jaw. Trust requires the same and adds a steadfast determination to walk forward regardless of the circumstances. Simply put, trust begins where faith ends and willfully enforces it in the face of the daily grinding and ungracious opposition of un-grace. Faith is a declaration. Trust is a determination. Faith is a statement of belief in God that is intended to bring focus to life. Trust is a statement of confidence in God in spite of being disillusioned with life—and perhaps even with God. Faith is a starting point, a port of departure. Trust is the course by which I sail through the heavy weather of life's storms.

My walk through the neighborhood continued. We were on the homestretch. I was headed for the safety of my chair in the den, while Honey contemplated her dog bed under the table.

I kept a brisk pace, my cadence a determined message reinforcing my will. I guarded my strengths and set sentries to help me care for my weaknesses. Honey, the lion hunter, kept an eye out for the cat who had stalked us all evening. In an odd, yet gracious gift, her furrowed brow, tightly curled tail, chiseled profile, and confident prance were a mirror of my resolve to enjoin grace in ungracious places.

## Something to Consider

What are your strengths and corresponding weaknesses? How aware are you of Satan's stalking approach at un-guarded moments?

I think the audacity of Satan to attack my greatest strengths and most profound weaknesses—after all, this is not where I would attack if I were him—is tied to my famil-iarity with, and acceptance of, my strengths and weaknesses.

Cats—all cats, but especially the great cats, like lions—are hunters equipped for stealth, surprise, and steady patience. As incredulous as it seems back home in the safety of my chair, I often miss the fact that the devil has anything to do with the miserable losses I suffer. It is as though his catlike temptation is so quiet and unassuming in its nor-malcy that I conclude the ensuing battle is a civil conflict between God and me or, worse yet, an internal conflict between me and me. I must not fail to realize the real field of battle draws clear lines between God and Satan. The conflict is bipartisan, not civil or independent. I, the new creation and child of God, am on his side. He has equipped me for every battle through the power of the Holy Spirit.

# MEDITATION
## & RESPONSE

*Father, it is tiresome being stalked. I must always be on guard. What a sobering reminder that this battlefield is not my home or ultimate place of rest.*

*You have given me all that is necessary to defend myself in life and comprehend godliness (see 2 Peter 1:3). What a great testimony of your grace in ungracious places.*

*Father, I would not be so cocky as to assume this issue of trust I struggle against has been whipped. I feel a bit like the folks in the Bible who asked for another miracle, but in all honesty, I feel as though I need something more to get me over the hump of distrust.*

*I feel awkward telling you that I am tripping on trust again, Father. But you tell me to bring my concerns to you, and you stipulate no exclusions. So I bring my ungracious struggle to you and ask that you shine your grace into the darkness of my distrust.*

*Thanks, Papa.*

# four

# Trust God? No Way!

D o you ever wonder if God is everything he claims to be? As I have told you, the great struggle of my life is trusting God, but this is not an acceptable sin to discuss at church. The Christian community is tolerant of a wide range of sins and their consequences, not so as to condone them, but to understand and address them. However, failing to trust God is not on the list of tolerated sins. Questioning God is ungracious.

Nevertheless, trusting God has been my Achilles heel. I have kept my failure under wraps, put up a good front, and talked a good game with almost flawless execution. Like everyone else, I have sung with gusto, "Trust and obey, for there's no other way to be happy in Jesus, but to trust and obey."

But when I get away from the crowd, lay aside my Sunday school answers, drop my religious facade, and look at my relationship with God, I must admit my resistance to trusting him. My opinion has been that it would be best if God stayed on his side of the universe and I stayed on mine.

To remain safe from this capricious deity and escape his notice, an even more ungracious and downright heretical goal guided my approach to life. By doing what is right, tagging all the religious bases, parroting all the correct theological perspectives, and leading a spiritually disciplined life, I attempted to create and maintain a safe distance from this unpredictable, dangerous God.

It took some time for me to realize that performing for God and doing the right things wouldn't mask my trust issue. It's silly to me now to even think that I could hide my feelings from him, but I wanted so badly to keep from admitting such a heinous mistrust that I suppressed its existence and intensity.

Ultimately, I confessed my distrust to God, which was emotionally liberating in that it got the issue onto the table for discussion. But that's as far as confession took me. In fact, once I admitted my problem it flared up with greater intensity than ever before. Perhaps the Lord wanted to make sure I understood the scope of my skepticism. If that was the case, it worked. I told him regularly that I was sinking in a stormy sea of distrust and that unless he intervened, calmed the waters, and reached out to me as he did to Peter on the Sea of Galilee, I would most certainly drown on my side of the pitching universe, and he would be to blame.

God began to answer my prayers, not as I anticipated, but as he intended. I remained in my tunnel of uncertainty. While I could see a light at the end of my dark passage, I could only hope it was God bringing a lantern to guide me out of my despair and not the cold, callous train of his divine supremacy coming to run me down in the night like a grasshopper on the track.

Every so often I caught fleeting glimpses of him. I had hoped for a dynamic revelation that would put my heart at complete rest and eliminate my distrust. After all, that's the way I would do it if I were God and he were me. But he had a better plan.

Some months after I placed my distrust before God, I was answering questions following a lecture at Nashville's Brentwood Academy. I have no recollection of the question, but in order to make my point, I turned to the whiteboard and wrote, "You will never learn to trust God until your faith in God has been challenged." Whether I adequately answered the student's question or not became of secondary importance. I realized God was addressing my distrust. Written before me on the whiteboard—literally in black and white—was the first installment of his answer.

I had a working definition of faith—"confidence in God and his ability"—but I had no definition for trust. The words written before me gave meaning to my experience and enabled me to understand the crisis of faith that had plagued my Christian life for years. Trust picks up where faith has to be applied. Trust means confidence in God even when it appears as though he isn't trustworthy. In order to trust God, my faith in God would have to experience crisis. And it did—a perpetual state of it.

As the words on the whiteboard burned into my mind, I saw meaning in my struggle for trust. The ungraciousness and dishonorable anxiety plaguing my spiritual world were purposeful. I sensed God chipping away at the distance between us. Seeing him graciously take the initiative to address my ungracious brawl with distrust was enough to begin building my trust in God.

Months became years, and I continued clinging tenaciously to what I knew of trusting God: confidence in him even though he appears untrustworthy. Time and again this accurately summarized what I seemed to be experiencing. As each wave of distrust crested and loomed over me, I tried to convey to God what was occurring in my heart.

I had paddled alone through my sea of skepticism for a long time, and there was still a lot of open water in front of me. I knew without a doubt that my ability to trust was one rogue wave of disillusionment away from drowning. I knew as well that God was the only rescue vessel around. Meanwhile, the storm of life lashed angrily on.

On Easter Sunday, 1987, I was in my beloved 1971 orange VW Beetle heading home from an early errand. I was following another car down a residential street and watched in horror as a squirrel made a break for the other side of the street. He didn't make it. The car in front of me hit him. I quickly pulled over and ran back to the injured squirrel. His hind legs were hurt badly, and he was bleeding internally. I carefully picked him up and carried him over to the thick carpet of St. Augustine grass in front of an unknown home and knelt down beside him.

His muscles were hard, and his sharp claws scratched into the skin of my hands and wrists, drawing copious amounts of blood. His ears were laid back against his head in a display of uncertainty, and there was terror in his shiny black eyes.

I searched in vain for some memory of what to do for a creature in such pain and fear. I wanted to touch him and comfort him, but he shrank in terror from each move I made. I spoke to him softly with reassuring words straight from my aching, empathetic heart—but to no avail. My godlike, imposing form hovering so close overhead grated against everything within his squirrel upbringing.

After a few moments, pulling himself on his belly across the grass, dragging his back legs behind him, the squirrel crawled toward a hedge, leaving me kneeling on the lawn in grief at the scenario I was sure would follow.

I looked down at my hands, streaked with his blood and mine, and then back out at the wounded squirrel dragging his fleeing heart from my presence. In an instant, the scene changed. Suddenly, I was in the place of the squirrel, wounded, dragging myself by my fingernails from the presence of a God who hovered over me. Terrified, I looked into the eyes of this figure kneeling beside me, and for the first time caught a glimpse of God's heart. Switching alternately between my godlike image to the squirrel and my horrified, squirrel-like condition before God, I comprehended God's thoughts. Staring at the blood on my hands as I knelt in the grass, I saw God kneeling over my fleeting life, considering the blood shed from his hands.

I understood. God ran across the universe between us, stopped me in my tracks on Easter Sunday, 1987, and was now making every effort to convey his heart to me. Praise God, I understood!

I got back in my car and headed for home. The stronghold of my distrust had fallen before God's pummeling grace. Gratitude welled up where threat sat stagnant. Joy invaded the armory of my fear and doubt.

Perhaps the most significant change I recognized was a subtle one. God didn't say anything about it while I processed the event of Easter morning, but a few days later, as I was revisiting the experience and discussing it with God, I noticed I addressed him as "Father" for the first time. As long as he was on the other side of the universe, he was God. But when he condescended to bring his grace, kneel beside me in my state of un-grace, and share his heart with me, he took on the visage of Father. I encountered the "Abba Father" Jesus spoke about and discovered he is trustworthy.

What an Easter! I expected him to be at churches around the world, admiring all the new clothes purchased in his honor. But he met me on an asphalt street, in an unknown yard, unshaven, unshowered, bleeding, on the most unlikely

41

of mornings, with a special four-legged emissary sent to assist in revealing his heart to me.

The Bible says the enemy accuses me before God on a regular basis, and this is absolutely true. But what I must not forget is that the enemy also accuses God before me whenever circumstances provide the opportunity. Satan has what seems to be a one-track mind: *How can I make God look bad in this situation?*

As he rants and raves, pitching my lifeboat around like a stick of wood, it *appears* as though God is less than he claims to be. It *appears* that he really has lost track and let me slip through a crack in heaven's bureaucracy. It *appears* that Satan has found a loophole God didn't anticipate and that I am indeed adrift in a sea of isolation. My confidence in God—faith—*appears* to be without foundation.

But this is the arena where trust thrives and spars with the deceiver and his deceptions. In this tempest, trust declares confidence in Father even though it *appears* he has abandoned ship.

Trust stands at the bowsprit of life's vessel, catching the spray from Satan's angry storm directly in the face, and declares, "I know whom I have believed and am persuaded that he is able." How is this? Because trust is the eye that sees through the mist and spray and ugliness of un-grace and into Father's heart of grace.

## Something to Consider

What is the ungracious situation you are in?

Like me, have you concluded your failure is too great for even God?

As I consider what I have learned of trust, I realize there is the notion that trusting God means sailing placidly through life's storms and not asking him the questions that seem too ungracious to voice to God. From this somewhat sane chair where I sit at the moment, I readily identify this notion as foolish. But in actual practice, I have suffered alone with my doubts, adhering to the belief that God neither knows nor cares. It isn't that he can't know what I'm struggling against, but that he chooses not to subject himself to the ungracious morass of my mess.

Omnipotence doesn't strike me as selective. Either God knows everything or he doesn't. And grace is either pervasive or it is not. Until I stripped away all the facades I had erected to protect my failure to trust and was honest with myself and God, he stayed his hand from uncovering the grace he had extended to me all along.

How much stripping do you have to do before you approach God with naked honesty?

## MEDITATION & RESPONSE

*Father. That is a great beginning! Thank you for making your name of preference, Father, slip so easily from my lips. It hasn't always been that way.*

*I celebrate the fact that you are trustworthy, but I still battle the resistance movement of my flesh, fighting to control my section of turf. I know the independent yearning I feel derives viability in the accusations Satan brings concerning your trustworthiness. I know there are battles yet to be fought, but I rejoice over the ground taken from the enemy's stronghold in my life.*

*Father, I realize that I do not recognize the need to trust unless I face a crisis of faith. In this moment of calm, I seize the lever of my will and choose to depend on you regardless of what comes my way.*

*My heart wants to trust you, and my desire is to courageously face the spiritual brawls that test my resolve to side with you. Father, I want to look at you and see your heart.*

*Thanks, Papa.*

# five

# Pain: The Black Knight

Have you noticed that pain and fear, like most special forces operations, use the darkness of night to gain the advantage during their attack?

In recent nights an old adversary has returned to joust with me for the hand of victory. He is a black knight on a gray horse who rides at dusk with an entourage of mealy-mouthed knaves. His allegiance is to no one in particular, but his true identity is unmistakable. Fear's face is under the black helmet with the slotted visor. With massive hands he grips his lance and hoists his shield. Behind his breast-plate is a heartless chest housing an unscrupulous soul.

For twenty years I have wrestled with undiagnosed physical pain. It started intermittently and became constant on

March 19, 1982. I have learned—the hard way mostly—what I can and can't do. I can't ride in a car for a long time; can't lie on my right side; can't sit next to my wife on the couch; can't make the bed (may be a blessing in disguise); can't bag the grass when I mow; and can't fold the clothes when they come out of the dryer. I might be able to struggle through folding the clothes, but don't you dare tell Dianne I said that.

Lately I can't sleep. Of all the twitching, wiggling, jerking, groaning, gritting, and flopping you've never seen the like. A few nights ago even Honey, the dog, who gets to lie on the bed until "lights out," raised her head and stared at me with yellow eyes as if to say, "Would you quit squirming?"

And you know what? There's not much happening in my neighborhood at 3:00 A.M. When I get up at that hour, half my day has already happened by breakfast. I sometimes wonder if I ought to even eat breakfast. Maybe an early lunch would be more appropriate.

The normal bedtime ritual is to swallow my vitamins, check the doors, set the alarm, and dive toward my pillow. (You should see lots of running and intensity in this ritual. I must get to bed no later than second place in order to claim my spot before Dianne and the dog begin encroaching.)

But recently I have been accosted by the dark rider. As I contemplate lying down, the spasms that will certainly begin, the tossing, the dark room in the wee hours of the morning, and the clouds of fatigue, Fear lowers his lance, or swings his mace, or stabs at me with the point of his sword. And I feel ill equipped to fight, standing there in my robe.

But fight I must, or be run through and bludgeoned. King David said to Goliath, "You come to me with a sword, a spear, and a javelin, but I come to you in the name of the LORD of hosts, the God of the armies of Israel, whom you have taunted. The LORD does not deliver by sword or spear; for the battle is the LORD's" (1 Sam. 17:45, 47).

Fear ominously jockeys for position. I know from years of experience that his accomplice, Pain, will not miss his appointment with my bedtime. I will come to blows with Fear. Pain will land hard, burning punches on my body.

The outlook is grim, and the enemy taunts, "Sleep is illusive. The mattress is really a rack, and you are my prisoner. Morning is hours away, and I own the night and its depths. You are mine."

But the fight does not belong to Fear as he claims. The battle is the Lord's. He is able. I may *feel* ill equipped, wandering the dark house in my pj's, but I am clothed with the armor of God and armed with the sword of the Spirit.

The dark knight has his gnarly knaves, but I am surrounded by warriors from the kingdom of light and supplied by God himself, who is love—and "perfect love casts out fear" (1 John 4:18). My body takes the brunt of the battle, while my spirit and soul form an ever-tightening alliance with the Lord. I may lose sleep, but I find that Father is more than sufficient. I may take a beating in the fight, but the battle belongs to him. Fear jousts about, but the "joy of the Lord is [my] strength" (Neh. 8:10).

Fear. Pain. Darkness. Sleeplessness. Disorientation. Dread. These do not lend themselves to a nice, neat, surgical battle. On the contrary. It is a grueling, bludgeoning, hand-to-hand, pummeling, spitting, kicking street fight so ungracious it feels dishonorable. But there is no dishonor in scrapping to infuse grace into the un-grace of a butcher's blitz.

The dark knight and his knaves may boast that they own the night, but Father promises he will give us his treasures in the darkest hours (Isa. 45:3a).

## Something to Consider

I hope you know by now I love you, otherwise I wouldn't be so candid. I know you too encounter the dark rider and have bouts with Pain and Fear. I shout encouragement to you.

Fear may not be assaulting the drawbridge of your castle at this time, but that's only the calm before the storm. Either he or Pain or one of their allies will come strutting his stuff. Don't even think of trying to take him yourself. The battle is the Lord's, and the hand of victory is yours.

It took several days before I could gather a cogent plan of attack I could execute when awakened from a sound sleep by the vicelike grip of Pain. But determining what to do before I went to bed eventually built a response mechanism I was able to put in motion.

Having a plan counteracted the disorientation of the middle of the night. I flanked Fear with a small passage of Scripture I kept ready night and day:

> He made darkness His hiding place, His canopy around
> Him.
> He sent from on high, He took me;
> He drew me out of many waters.
> He delivered me from my strong enemy,
> And from those who hated me, for they were too
> mighty for me.
> They confronted me in the day of my calamity,
> But the LORD was my stay.
> He brought me forth also into a broad place;
> He rescued me, because He delighted in me.
>
> Psalm 18:11a, 16–19

As for pain, it is relentless; but Father is constant.

What issue are you facing that might become manageable if you meditated on a small passage of Scripture and determined to do whatever was necessary to remember that Father is constant?

# MEDITATION
## & RESPONSE

*Father, I thank you that you are constant, that you are the same every day, that you are unflappable, suffer no surprises, and are without shadow.*

*They say that pain makes cowards of us all, and that is true. But my strength comes from you, and you are victorious.*

*Father, I'm not much to look at. I'm scuffed and hollow-eyed, scarred and limping. I'm in no shape to do much dancing after a night of fighting. But I celebrate the victory you have won and am proud to be part of the campaign to conquer these final outposts of my flesh. I declare, to all who will listen, your grace is well-suited to ungracious places.*

*It is quite a journey we are on.*

*Thanks, Papa.*

## six

# Failure (Is It Fatal?)

Overnight we collected about an inch of ice, and then Old Man Winter finished off with an inch of dry snow. It looked more like Detroit than Fort Worth. After canceling work for the office staff, I stepped out to put my tire chains on the VW Bug. After much consternation, I decided I had changed tire sizes since I last used the chains in the winter of '77, so I abandoned the chain project and went in the house to find something hot to drink.

With a cup of coffee in my belly and a kiss from Dianne on my lips, I pointed the Bug in the general direction of the deserted office to prepare for an upcoming conference. The normally compliant VW was not happy and kept complaining about condensation in his gas tank—not something I wanted to deal with at the time. So in my stubbornness, I figured he'd get over it and mushed on toward the office.

The office was indeed abandoned, as were most of the thoroughfares of Cowtown. Relishing the solitude, I began praying that the Lord would guide my preparation for the impending conference. Several hours later—and no closer to inspiration—I felt abandoned in my solitude.

It seemed as if the doors to heaven had been locked and the windows barred. I listened for even a still small voice, a gentle whisper, an impression, but all was quiet on the heavenward front.

Late in the afternoon I decided to go home via the dry cleaners. The Bug had gotten sicker as the day progressed and was no longer just dying at stop lights; he was also lurching down the straightaways in intermittent death throes. This is not a good condition to be in, especially with ice on the streets and fools out on the roads—yours truly excepted of course.

While getting into the car with the cleaning, I whacked my head on the edge of the roof, knocked my hat over my eyes, tilted my glasses, dropped some cleaning, and slipped on the ice. I meant to say what the great philosopher Popeye declared, "I've had all I can stands; I can't stands no more," but it didn't quite come out that way. I totally lost it in a screaming, stomping, angry-at-God fit that lasted about fifteen seconds. Then there was silence, heavy silence.

All day long the devil had been assaulting the ramparts of my life's castle. All day long I had successfully battled against the enemy of my soul. Then, in a moment of inattentiveness, I failed. Throughout the day I had waged a noble battle only to let victory slip through my fingers at the last minute.

It was about midnight before I could sit down by the fire and regroup. Oh sure, I'd confessed my sin to the Lord, but I was still raw inside. I needed a salve for my soul, a haven for my mind, a respite from my wounded emotions—so I retreated to God's Word. Mark 16:7 surfaced: The angel at the empty tomb said, "Go, tell His disciples and Peter. . . ." That was the phrase I needed: "and Peter."

God had his angel single out one disciple. One follower well-acquainted with grief over his sin. One close friend languishing in the debacle of failure. One man whose eyes were bloodshot for reasons he'd rather no one else knew about. One soul sitting alone in a dark room, staring at the dying embers of his fire. One disciple living in heaviness and silence, weighted with the burden of his defeat and embarrassment.

The angel delivered the message to the visitors at the empty tomb just as he had been instructed: "Make a special point of telling Peter that Jesus wants him to meet him in Galilee." And the words Jesus instructed the angel to deliver at the tomb endured through the annals of time to another wounded and failure-shamed disciple.

There is no un-grace, no debacle of ungraciousness profound enough to shorten the reach of grace. There is no distance so great or darkness so deep that Father's light is dimmed. Nothing can separate us from the love of God (Rom. 8:38–39), not even the ungraciousness of failure.

God doesn't erase failure. He doesn't fill the silence with angels singing. He doesn't extract us from the tribulation of the world. But he does declare unabashedly and without reservation that we are his. If he went to hell to get us in the first place, he will not allow failure to steal us away, sin to separate us from him, or embarrassment to loosen his grip on us.

Failure isn't easy to talk about, live with, or get over. I suppose that is why they call it failure. But, as Sir Winston "the bulldog" Churchill said, "Failure is never fatal." However, it can be incapacitating if you don't accept Father's invitation to rejoin him in the noble cause of grace.

**Something to Consider**

Father hammered home a benchmark point earlier in
our journey. There is nothing you can do that will enhance
or tarnish his opinion of you. Let that sink into the crevices
of everything you have learned about God and yourself.
Is that what you believe, or is it simply a point underlined
on the page before you?

I was talking with Father several days ago about another
failure and the disappointment I, and the person I offended,
felt because I did not do what was expected of me. As I listened, I realized that disappointment comes when an expec-
tation is not met.

This prompted me to ask, "Father, what do you expect
of me?" His answer was swift and fairly blunt. "Pres, I
have no expectations of you. Therefore, it is impossible
for you to disappoint me."

God is extremely interested in what I do, and, in fact,
I have been created to do good works (Eph. 2:10). But while
this is a goal on God's agenda for me, it is not an expec-
tation. Father accepts me, and loves me, and thinks the
world of me because of who I am, not because of what I
do or fail to do.

## MEDITATION
### & RESPONSE

> *Father, it is more fun to bring you the victo-
> ries, successes, and accolades than it is to haul
> my failures and sins in and dump them on the
> floor.*
>
> *I do understand—although I'm not sure I
> fully comprehend—that you think no more*

*highly of me when I perform well, and your belief in me is not lowered when I fail. Adopting your attitude toward me is the harder part of the equation, but that is my intent.*

*Father, I bring my moments of grace and un-grace to you. Thank you for loving me, forgiving me, and not flinching when you see me coming. The smile on your face when you think of me is an encouragement my soul feeds on and my spirit takes refuge in.*

*Thanks, Papa.*

# Grace in Gloomy Places

# seven

# Is "Sorry" Good Enough?

When you apologize for some dastardly deed—or some not-so-dastardly deed—is your apology good enough? I have felt for as long as I can remember that it isn't. If forgiveness is to be mine, I have to work for it. Perform. Show my contrition and shame and prove I am genuinely sorry. Only after this penance is done can I regain the standing I have lost.

My philosophy has been that somewhere between the small matters, where a sincere apology is enough, and the larger sins is a place that requires more than "I'm sorry" affords. It is an imbalance that morphs and moves based upon circumstances, emotion, and perception. The decisions that transport me to this place render a shame more profound than "I'm sorry" will cover.

There are consequences to sin, but I'm not talking about consequences. I'm talking about falling out of favor and what it takes to regain that loss. Any important relationship that possesses the potential to fall short carries with it the potential to lose favor when I sin and cross into that fuzzy no-man's-land between a small matter and a big deal.

Dianne and I just purchased a used motorcycle from a friend we call Rodeo Bob. I am tickled to have the machine, but this pales in comparison to the lesson I learned while in pursuit of the bike.

I blew the negotiation in royal fashion. Praise God Bob understands my fleshly foibles and is a man of grace. Bob and Dianne and I met on a Saturday morning to discuss the bike. I was not certain I wanted a motorcycle, and Bob was not 100 percent sure he wanted to be without one. We agreed to take a few days to pray and think. I promised to call Bob on Monday.

Two days later I called to give Bob the good news that he had sold his hobby to us. Problem was, Rodeo Bob was still uncertain. He asked if he could call on Wednesday with his final decision. "I just love this bike," were his parting words.

Two hours before bedtime on Wednesday I had not heard from Bob and was anxious. So I decided to help the decision-making process with a telephone call. I got Bob's answering machine and left a message telling him we were excited about the bike and hoped he had good news for us when he called me back.

After I hung up I recognized that I had boxed Bob in. I took advantage of him with the message I left on his answering machine. Deciding not to sell the bike would require that he disappoint his friends. That's not fair. But worse yet, I acted independently of God. Instead of trusting him to give Bob the same guidance he gave us, I assumed responsibility and crafted a narrow path of response for Bob in order to get what I wanted.

I felt genuine conviction. I had taken advantage of a friend and used my own strength to play God's role and get what I desired for myself. I had failed and blown it with God and Bob.

I called Bob, confessed, and apologized. I offered to let him out of the deal. He was incredibly gracious. And then I went to the den and fell on my knees before God, confessing my independence. I told him I was sorry for my sin—a major infraction by my estimation. I knelt alone in the dark den, feeling shame for my behavior, wondering how to regain my standing with God, and fearing the consequences of my actions. Theologically, I knew I was forgiven, but experientially and emotionally I was haunted by the certitude of what I believed: "Sorry isn't good enough."

In an intensity close to panic, I racked my mind to figure out what I could do to restore my lost favor and hedge the consequences of falling into the hands of an angry God. A motorcycle provided God with too many horrific options for getting even with me. After all, you can be killed or maimed riding a motorcycle. What would God require to reestablish my standing with him? A lost leg? Paralysis? The options were dizzying. My failure couldn't be discounted. My emotional history corroborated my belief that God is harsh, rigid, and unforgiving. While he might be merciful, he is not lenient.

But in the midst of my anxiety and condemnation, I heard Father's unmistakable voice in my thoughts. *Pres, "Sorry" is good enough for me. I don't care what you think or feel about it. I know your heart. Yes, you blew it, but you have not fallen out of my favor. That is not possible. You know that. You teach it all the time. You have fallen out of favor with yourself. Don't live there and fail to trust me again. I accept you totally, and it is time you base your self-acceptance on my standard, not on your performance. Have a good time with the bike.*

I jumped up and called Bob. "Bob, you won't believe what happened. I just discovered that 'Sorry' is good enough. Whether the bike ever makes it to my garage or not, the negotiation has been worth it!"

## Something to Consider

Have you realized it is not possible to fall out of favor with your heavenly Father? No matter what you do, while there are consequences to sin, one of them is *not* losing your standing with him.

Underlying my belief that "Sorry" is not good enough is the assumption that God is out to get even with me. If that is true, then grace is actually the un-grace of tit for tat, forgiveness is a misnomer—it is actually justice—and the consequence of sin is really the retribution of a capricious deity.

Does God discipline his children? Yes. Are there consequences for sin? Yes. Does God seize the intensity of unpleasant circumstances to deliver important messages to us? Yes. But if you sort through all the details associated with each of these scenarios, at their core you will encounter a loving Father who is taking advantage of every opportunity to communicate his love and demonstrate his heart for you.

Does God punish us in anger? No. Does God seek to get even with us? No. Is God disappointed in us? No. Is God disgusted with the way we behave? No. At the core of each of these scenarios is an angry judge.

As you evaluate the last two paragraphs, be careful to do so from the perspective of the New Testament Jesus Christ, God incarnate, and not the Old Testament God of retribution.

Don't get me wrong. The entire Bible, both Old and New Testaments, is the inspired, infallible Word of God.

I am not discounting or discrediting a portion of the Scripture because I don't like the message it delivers. But we must not blur the division between the Old and New Testaments. The pages you and I idly flip between the Old and New Testaments cost Jesus Christ his life.

God says he inaugurated a new plan through the work of Jesus Christ's death on the cross. While the emotional intensity of my story was significant, and my offense to Bob was real, the greatest error in my approach to recovery from sin was believing I had to do something to get right with God.

God was gracious to me in his response to my confession and angst-driven apology. He might just as easily have told me that if this was the way I wanted to handle the situation, I should get off my knees, take the pickup truck, go buy a calf, and bring it home for a sin offering and burnt sacrifice.

Either we are in right standing with God through Christ or we are not. Either the work of Christ exists in the perpetuity of grace and the new covenant, or we live in the grim, ungracious uncertainty of sometimes having God's favor and sometimes not.

In negotiating my deal for the motorcycle, I discovered my theology was insufficient for the ungraciousness of my life. What about you? On which side of Christ's finished work at Calvary are you living?

## MEDITATION
### & RESPONSE

*Father, that is a pointed and troubling question: "On which side of Christ's finished work at Calvary am I living?" I know what* the answer is supposed to be, but I'm not convinced that's the answer I'm giving.

On the one hand, I am sobered by the thought that I could thumb my nose at Jesus by the theology I manifest in approaching life. On the other hand, I am grateful to you. I am a New Testament believer who often adopts an Old Testament perspective. Thank you for stress-testing my belief system and not allowing me to live with this incongruity. Were it not for this tension I feel, I would have a limited advantage in grasping the full import of your grace to me through Christ.

Papa, my heart wants desperately to do what is right, what is pleasing to you, and what honors you. I know my actions don't bear this out sometimes. Words escape me in expressing my deep appreciation to you. It would have been so easy for you to base your opinion of me on my performance, or lack thereof. Thank you for giving me a new heart and filling me with the Holy Spirit. Thank you for giving me the mind of Christ and for writing your laws on my heart instead of hanging them around my neck or beating me over the head with them.

I am motivated by your grace. And I am continually amazed that no matter what state of ungraciousness and sin I find myself

*embroiled in, your grace abounds all the more.
It is obvious you have much more in mind for
me than simply changing the way I act. Thank
you. I have felt I was more than the sum total
of my behavior, but I am easily confused.
Your grace is an endorsement that you see
more potential in me than I often see in myself.*

*Thank you, Papa.*

# eight

# Insecurity: A Sticky Morass

When enmeshed in the throes of insecurity and inferiority, have you ever wondered what it will take to obtain that elusive sensation of security? Recently I was at a meeting with a number of colleagues from around North America. The week was filled with the success stories of dynamite programs, promising ministries, new insights, and key revelations. It was a tremendous week.

On the last night of the conference, I was talking with a close friend over dinner. As we reminisced about the meeting highlights and compared notes, I said, "Do you ever wonder if you have really found the key? Whether you have gotten the message, are doing effective ministry work, and are really on the right track?"

Without hesitation my friend replied, "In all honesty, I'm struggling big-time. I'm ready to hear a story or two about how one of these guys spent the week in the ditch. I wonder if anybody else is having a weak financial period, or if any of these sister offices has had a conference that was a bust. I wonder if anyone else has had their key materials plagiarized or feel like they have spent more time with their lawyer than they have with the Lord. Yeah, I've been wondering a lot. In fact, I've been wondering since about Wednesday."

I've run the business end of our ministry since 1985. That is long enough to know that everyone has slow spots and downturns, canceled conferences, books that go out of print, and key employees that leave. Intellectually, I am secure that we have a fine ministry that is doing great work. Spiritually, I believe the Lord has shown us some invaluable, life-changing, essential truths and keys to Christian living. And pragmatically, I am confident that everyone encounters a dilly of a storm every now and then. My dinner buddy knows these things as well, but that doesn't change the fact that we were getting pitched around by our emotions, feeling insecure and inferior compared to the stories we heard all week.

Insecurity. It can drag you down into a sticky morass of self-condemnation, self-degradation, and self-doubt. It can cause you to lash out indiscriminately and irrationally at those closest to you. Or it can motivate an assessment of the foundation upon which you have built. In this scenario, the question becomes, "Does the foundation hold or quake?"

A good shaking can be one of the most inspiring, beneficial things that can happen to you. Once you see that Father is committed to weaning you away from dependence upon the flesh, a tumult tremendous enough to shake the flesh and settle your spiritual foundation can inspire great faith, which is nothing more than confidence in Father.

I'm glad the Bible doesn't read like my memories of this conference. If Genesis to Revelation told only success stories and recounted only victory marches, I would be in serious trouble. On the contrary, the heroes of our faith give candid, transparent reports of getting tangled up in the affairs of the world and running their lives into the ditch. But they also share the perspective they gained during those ungracious periods.

King David, a man well acquainted with all life can bring and blessed with phenomenal power as monarch of Israel, writes, "Lead me to the rock that is higher than I" (Ps. 61:2b). He knew power was a narcotic that would addict him to his flesh instead of his God. He knew the circumstances of life could quickly turn sour. But he knew there was a rock higher than himself, and in ungracious places, he called for the author of grace to lead him to a higher place.

I think others who have gone before us and recorded their life-reports would agree with David. Daniel and Joseph, both of whom were the number two men in their kingdoms, realized that success was a vapor. They would echo David, who said elsewhere, "And besides You, I desire nothing on earth" (Ps. 73:25). Moses learned in a hurry that his reputation as Pharaoh's son wasn't where his resources resided. They were taken from him in a moment. He twice encountered the Rock that was higher than himself. Abraham too, for all of his wealth, armies, herds, and extended entourage, conceded the impossibilities of his own abilities and looked forward with faith to the coming of the Rock.

How tempting it is to evaluate the visible results—glowing reports, glorious stories of successes, miracles recounted—and lay ourselves open to the enemy's suggestion that we don't measure up. Insecurity. The devil is always trying, isn't he? He's hoping against hope that he can undermine the security we have in Father.

Situations that spin off insecurity are unavoidable, but what we do in response is within our control. Insecurity can be a morass or a motivation. I choose the latter, and in the process echo the conviction of a man whom I admire and look forward to meeting one day: "Father, lead me to the Rock that is higher than I."

### Something to Consider

Do you realize that no rock, other than Christ, is high enough to satisfy what drives you? No rock is deep enough, other than the Rock, to anchor you with the security you long for? It is tough to remember with Satan incessantly screaming otherwise. But it is the truth, and what we do with Satan's posturing and Father's declaration is our choice.

So what will it take to create the security you dream of?

## MEDITATION
### & RESPONSE

*Father, it is so tempting to look at the circumstances around me to determine whether we are winning or losing. I keep forgetting that this life is not about me and my story. It is about you, and I am a supporting actor to you, the leading man.*

*This being the case, while my limited perception of the battle around me is an impor-*

tant concern of yours—and mine—it has little to do with whether you are victorious, I am secure, and we win the war in the end.

Father, I return to what Paul said, "For to me, to live is Christ and to die is gain" (Phil. 1:21). That is inspiration to me, Father. No. On second thought, it is more than inspiration. It is perspective.

Thanks, Papa.

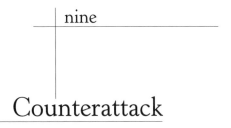

## nine

# Counterattack

J ust a few weeks ago I walked into the house late in the
evening after being delayed by mechanical problems
on a flight into the Dallas-Fort Worth airport. As I
looked into my wife, Dianne's, eyes, I knew instantly that
something was wrong.

"Your mom is in the hospital downtown. She was having chest pains, and the doctor put her into the Coronary
Care Unit at Harris Hospital."

How's that for a homecoming?

Sure enough, tests revealed that Mom has a 70 percent
blockage in one of her arteries, which has created low
blood pressure, chest pain, and fatigue. In addition to this,
her heart is not beating rhythmically, necessitating a blood

thinner to reduce the chance of the blood coagulating within the heart, clotting, and causing a stroke, the very thing her mom died from.

The C.C.U. is quite a testimony to medicine's advances in caring for patients who have heart problems. The rooms tend to be utilitarian with lots of wires, instrumentation, and outlets. Mom's room even had a camera installed so she could be visually monitored at the nurse's station. Unlike the other hospital wings I'm familiar with, all of the personnel on the floor were at least RNs, which speaks loudly of the critical issues handled on the fourth floor.

There are no good fixes for conditions such as Mom's. For all the medical advancement and sophistication, the fact remains that there is only so much science can do for hearts with blockages and arrhythmia.

After my third night sitting in the C.C.U. waiting room, I went home, collapsed onto the couch, and turned on a rerun of *Star Trek*. During a commercial I channel surfed and landed on a TV preacher. The flamboyant orator was proclaiming the power of faith to move the hand of God and give us what is "our right"—health, wealth, cars, exemption from pain. "Whatever we desire is ours. We are King's kids, and we should settle for nothing less," he preached. I flipped back to *Star Trek*.

But I thought of my mom and my hopes and prayers for her health and well-being. And I considered the message of the well-meaning preacher. When weighed against Jesus' lifestyle and the balance of Scripture, the TV theology was selfish, shallow, and wanting. It created hunger and thirst, but for the wrong things. The preacher's theology espoused the doctrine of entitlement, sought heaven on earth, and positioned God as the head of a welfare state. The indignity of associating entitlement and welfare with God's grace made me angry. What an insidious package of nicely wrapped theological tripe Satan had prepared and delivered via the TV preacher. Predictably, he had prepared it for my moment of vulnerability.

When someone you love or some issue of importance hangs in the balance, the enemy is quick to deceive, mislead, disguise himself as an angel of light, quote Scripture, and offer the kingdoms and enticements of this world as relief from the ungraciousness of the moment. God does not work that way, and he has made it clear in his Word. But in his counterattack, the enemy will be quick to accuse God of being less than his loving self. "Anything to tarnish grace and discredit God!" Surely this must be the mission statement hanging on the lobby wall of hell.

God is on his throne, and he has heard every last prayer that you and I have prayed. Only eternity will accurately reveal the divine length to which he has gone to answer our prayers and comfort us in our concerns.

But the fact remains that what I just referred to as "the divine length" doesn't always look like we want it to. Such is the nature of grace in ungracious places. Satan will seize the disappointment caused by the difference between our expectations and God's manifestations and assert that God is mean, capricious, aloof, petty, and unloving.

Satan is an opportunistic liar! Whatever God decides to do is anchored in grace. The fact is that God's ways are higher than yours or mine. Restated: There are many of God's actions that we are incapable of understanding. When we cannot find Father's hand, we must trust his heart of grace. In contrast, Satan is low enough to use the ungrace of heartache as his opportunity to take ungracious advantage and strike a low blow—at you, at me, and especially at God.

Difficulty is not necessarily a sign that God is angry or that you have done something wrong. Jesus said, "In the world you have tribulation" (John 16:33). It only seems prudent that we prepare ourselves for those difficulties everyone will have, whether lost or saved. We must lean on him more than ever before. Confidently we must rest in him, on him, and against him. After all, he finished the warning in John 16:33 with a declaration: "I have overcome the world."

## Something to Consider

When you find yourself in the throes of the battle, important issues are at stake, and your soul is yanked from pillar to post, how will you stay focused on grace even though you are in an ungracious place?

David said, "I will remember my song in the night; I will meditate with my heart" (Ps. 77:6a). For David to remember his song at night, when he was struggling mightily, means he was singing it during the day when he was experiencing relative peace and tranquility. Pastor Bo Baker told me one time, "Son, God can cut a lot of wood with a sharp axe." Now is a good time to sharpen your focus on God's grace.

After a five-verse street fight with the demons of doubt, rejection, hopelessness, deception, loss, and anger, David offers a wise response for us to model: "I shall remember the deeds of the LORD; surely I will remember Your wonders of old. I will meditate on all Your work and muse on Your deeds" (Ps. 77:11–12).

What do you know of Father? That is an important question to answer. Sit down in the midst of your ungracious mess and take inventory. Consider his ways. Ponder his grace. Compare what the devil is suggesting against the person of Jesus Christ. Total up all the people who have died so you can live. Contemplate who you know that determined he would rather die than live without you.

After you have taken inventory of these considerations, answer the original question: What do you know of Father? Then, as David did, remember, meditate, and muse.

# MEDITATION
## & RESPONSE

*Father, I know you are faithful.*

*Thank you that you are not only with me but in me. It would be great if you were around, or close at hand, or simply keeping a watchful eye. But it is utterly fantastic that you are in me, bonded to me with an inseparable bond forged by Christ.*

*Sometimes when fear, or anger, or resentment—or any number of other things—seem closer to home than my real place in your kingdom, I wonder if I'm on my own because of the ungracious nature of my surroundings. It is an amazing testimony to your confidence and faithfulness that grace thrives in ungracious places.*

*Thank you, Papa.*

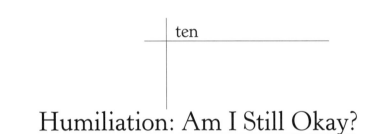

ten

# Humiliation: Am I Still Okay?

I was setting off for the grocery store last week and backed through—not out of—the garage door. My routine was off. Ordinarily I step out of the house and into the garage, open the garage door, get in the truck, and back out. But I decided that it would be good to take the dog with me.

Since the dog is prone to run off, and I wasn't in the mood to chase her, I didn't open the garage door first. I was planning to do that after the dog got in the truck. It was a workable plan; I just forgot to execute the "open the garage door" step, and the plan happened to have a low tolerance for missing that part.

Well, the dog isn't smart enough to know that what occurred wasn't standard procedure. Don't all masters gnash their teeth, hit their heads on the steering wheel, and walk around the truck raising their arms up and down saying, "Oh no!"?

Dianne knew better. She emerged from the house with her arms up in the air as well. "What happened? Oh, my soul! How did you do that?" You know, those were tough questions to answer: "Well, dear . . . you'll notice . . . calmly, calmly . . . that the dog is in the front seat of the truck . . . along with the shopping list for the grocery store. And, well . . . you see . . ."

It wasn't the most graceful show I've put on in my life. After I had gone to the store, I pulled the garage door back inside the garage and bent it back in the general direction of its original shape.

Later that night I sat on the patio thinking, *Nothing is really any the worse for wear. There's a dent in the door, and the truck has a scratch on the fender, but all in all everything is fine. I can fix the door tomorrow, and trucks are supposed to have scratches on their fenders.*

The neighborhood was enveloped in its late-night lull. Dianne was in the house asleep, and the dog was lying at my feet listening to whatever dogs listen to, but I was not in a lull, nor was I fine. I had performed poorly and done something stupid. I wasn't proud of Pres and didn't feel very acceptable. But as I sat on the patio, waiting for the adrenaline to clear out of my system so I could go to bed, the Lord began to remind me of how accepted I am.

How long has it been since you reminded yourself that there is nothing you can do—even backing through the garage door—that will make God accept you less? And how long since you've reflected on the fact that there is nothing you can do that will cause God to accept you more? How long since you've buckled down, focused on the truth, and determined to accept yourself as God does?

God's acceptance isn't conditional or performance based. He declared us accepted in Christ (Rom. 15:7) and makes no provision for changing his mind. Backing through garage doors is hard on doors, trucks, and perspective, but it has no effect on acceptance. The Lord reminded me that everything was okay—including me. While the paint on the truck is scratched, my acceptance is untarnished because it is based upon my identity in Christ.

The challenge is unmistakable: Line your perspective up with Father's opinion, not vice versa. The reminder is unalterable: Your acceptance doesn't go up and down based upon whether the garage door does.

## Something to Consider

Every one of us pursues love and acceptance. Minor catastrophes play havoc with our perspective and emotional well-being, but Father's acceptance of us is non-negotiable, unchanging, and unfazed. Why? Because his opinion of us is not formulated based on the way we perform. If we are in Christ, we are accepted.

Given this fact, the crises we face—spouses that go astray, rebellious children, financial pressure, job loss, death, loneliness, or, at the other end of the spectrum, roaring success, recognition, love, celebration, promotion, pride—are golden opportunities for us to see grace in ungracious places.

Yours is not the only perspective regarding the tangle of circumstances around you. What is Father's opinion about the place in which you find yourself?

# MEDITATION
## & RESPONSE

*Father, I give you the entanglement trip-ping me up. And yes, I do agree with you. My success is often more debilitating to the advance of your grace in my life than the wounds I receive from crashing into the ditch.*

*Better yet, Papa, I not only give you the things that trip me up, but I ask you to cut me loose from them. I've been caught in enough snags over the years to realize I will tear my shirt and rip my pants attempting to twist and turn and extricate myself.*

*I know your Word is sharp and able to pierce to the division between my soul and spirit. But what I need to know right now is, can you use your sword to cut me out of where I am?*

*Thanks, Papa.*

# Grace in
# Dangerous
# Places

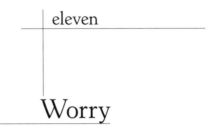

eleven

# Worry

I probably have a bit more research to do, but thus far, all my worries begin, "What if," and then proceed to contemplate various future scenarios, none of which I have any control over and all of which entice me to live tomorrow before I have finished trusting Christ for today. Worry assumes responsibility for something that is expressly in God's hands.

Jesus asked, "Will all your worries add a single moment to your life? . . . So do not worry about tomorrow; for tomorrow will care for itself. Each day has enough trouble of its own" (Matt. 6:27 TLB; 6:34 NASB).

There are two places in the Bible where people ask "what if" questions. In Genesis 50:15, Joseph's brothers begin to worry as they contemplate what Joseph might do to them now that their father has died. "When Joseph's brothers saw that their father was dead, they said, 'What if Joseph bears a grudge against us and pays us back in full for all the wrong which we did to him?'" And in the classic passage we are all familiar with, Moses worries about Israel following him: "What if they will not believe me or listen to what I say?" (Exod. 4:1). On this side of history, where we enjoy twenty-twenty hindsight, it is interesting to note that both Joseph's brothers and Moses asked intriguing questions, but they were hypothetical questions that never needed an answer or solution. It is appropriate to recognize the issues of tomorrow, but if we lose sight of what we know today, we have begun to worry.

The dictionary says worry is feeling undue care and anxiety, and while that is a good definition—after all, it made its way into the dictionary—who's to say when feeling anxious becomes undue? If your worst-case scenario begins unfolding, and you are ravaged by the ungraciousness of your dread, who's to say what an appropriate level of anxiety is versus an undue level?

The renowned Bible teacher Malcolm Smith says worry is fearing that God is not sufficient. I think that is a workable definition. Although the Bible doesn't talk much about worry, God does devote a number of verses in his Book to anxiety. Perhaps the most familiar is Paul's exhortation, "Be anxious for nothing" (Phil. 4:6). The passage from Matthew we referenced earlier is the Bible's lengthiest and most compelling discussion on anxiety delivered by Jesus during his Sermon on the Mount. Allow me to summarize his key points with this paraphrase: "Do not be anxious for your life, for what you will eat, what you will drink, or what you will wear. Consider the birds. Think about the flowers. Your Father watches over the birds, clothes the flowers, and cares more for you than he does for either birds or flowers. Why be anxious?" (see Matt. 6:25–34).

I can't help but wonder, as much as Jesus quoted the Old Testament, if he was trying to help his mountain-side audience understand and apply David's statement in the Psalms: "When my anxious thoughts multiply within me, your consolations delight my soul" (Ps. 94:19). The argument could be made that David did not face the ominous prospects we face—war, human rights abuse, computer viruses, infrastructure collapse, nuclear proliferation, terrorist threat—and thus makes an assertion that doesn't apply today. But then again, David spent a fair bit of time running for his life and dodging spears hurled by Israel's disgruntled and insecure monarch, King Saul.

I think we all face the temptation to believe our concerns are the gravest of all time and that no one has ever faced the pressures we face. Of course, in our rational moments, we know this is not the case, but the temptation persists nevertheless. Our heavenly Father knows the pervasiveness of this temptation and inspired David to say, "Even in the face of multiplying anxieties, your consolations— thoughts, comforting perspective, and encouragement— delight my soul."

This leads me to an observation: The wind chill today is 8 degrees. Off and on throughout the morning the sparrows have landed on my windowsill to eat the seed I put out for them. As nearly as I can determine, they do not seem any more anxious about today's cold than they were about yesterday's relative warmth.

In the flower bed below the windowsill the pansies seem unaffected by the ice storm and colder-than-normal temperatures enveloping North Texas. Their colors are as vibrant today as they were five weeks ago when the landlord planted them. They do not worry about God's provision; they bloom where they are planted.

Isaiah wrote, "Say to those with anxious heart, 'Take courage, fear not'" (Isa. 35:4). And I would add, consider the sparrows and the pansies. Doing so will bolster your courage and arm you against worry, because they are tangible, simple testimonies that God is sufficient for them and will be for you as well.

Determining to believe God and not yield to worry is not synonymous with sticking your head in the sand. It is wise to assess the circumstances in your life and consider the challenges you may face. Given the ungracious circumstances around us, this can be an arduous undertaking. But fretting, losing sleep, worrying, or yielding to anxiety does not help. Not only do these responses not add a single moment of comfort, they do not answer the challenges before you or take into consideration the promises of your heavenly Father to care for you.

Plan? Yes. Contemplate and consider? Yes. Evaluation is appropriate, but worry is not. Worry is built upon the false supposition that God is insufficient to handle your concerns, not to mention that it flies in the face of Father's counsel in Scripture.

God's consolations are before you. Your worry may become a reality, but it won't kill the sparrow on your windowsill, uproot the pansies in your flower bed, or diminish God's determination to take care of you today. Take courage. Father's grace is more profound than the potential ungraciousness proposed in your worry.

## Something to Consider

What do you think about when you lie awake?
What motivates the plans you are making?
If your heart had fingernails, would they be chewed off?

Before we consider what to do with worry, let me be clear about one thing: Trusting Christ to give you the victory over what worries you, only to find that your worry returns to the forefront of your thoughts, does not mean you are failing in your bid to be free of worry. Satan will continue to put thoughts of worry into your mind, as if you were a slot machine in Vegas, in hopes you will return to worrying and grant him the satisfaction of a jackpot of successful deception. The worrisome thoughts may return time and time again, and, while this is a major nuisance, you deal with each recurrence the same way you dealt with the first.

And how is it we deal with worry to begin with? Dealing with worry, or any other kind of burden you encounter, is a four-step process. First, you recognize: You recognize the thought as Satan's effort and, therefore, as a temptation. Second, you refuse: You refuse—with teeth-gritted determination and resolve—the option to consider his illegitimate offering. Third, you recall or reckon: You recall that Father has you and everything concerning you under control. Fourth, you rest: You rest in the truth by setting your mind—repeatedly and with great frequency—on God's truth with the tenacity of a cornered badger.

So you have permission right now to summon your worries to the front of your mind. Examine them. Do they begin with the hypothetical introduction of "what if"? Sure they do.

Now carefully and deliberately take the four steps above and tailor each to every worry plaguing you. If necessary, take some notes. The devil will not easily give up the turf he has gained through worry. You will revisit the four steps often. But this is okay. While you will struggle frequently and intensely against the ungraciousness of tomorrow's—or the next moment's—worries, you will frequently and intensely be reminded of Father's grace right now.

## MEDITATION
### & RESPONSE

*Father, I know you are sufficient! Your sufficiency is a theological concept I have adhered to for a long time. To do otherwise would be unchristian. That much I have learned. But I have lived otherwise, and that is certainly not indicative of you or your grace. I know you are sufficient for the big things, making everything right at the end of time and ensuring that the Earth keeps spinning. But it is the little things that the devil uses to entice me to live as though you are insufficient for each day's problems.*

*Father, I give you the big things and the little things, the things I can see and the things I can't see, the things I can predict and the surprises. I give you those around me, and I give you myself. I give you my hopes and dreams, and I give you this moment, and I ask that you enable me to trust you now.*

*If this happens, and I can trust you now, then when tomorrow arrives—regardless of what it holds—I will be prepared for whatever action your sufficiency will manifest to bolster my trust in you and lead me in the triumph of your grace in ungracious places.*

*Thanks, Papa.*

## twelve

# Anxiety

I was thigh deep in the murky waters of the Brazos River a few weeks ago fly-fishing for largemouth bass. As I worked my way around a brushy deadfall protruding into the river, I flipped my fly carefully under the branches hoping for the trademark attack of a violent and angry fish. Instead, what I saw gave my heart a start. The largest water moccasin I have ever encountered slithered its gray-black body off the deadfall and into the water with me.

For an instant there was a slight writhing as the poisonous reptile undulated its heavy body into the water. Only a small ripple remained marking its entrance. There was nothing to indicate its direction of travel.

It is a common misconception that water moccasins cannot bite and inject their venom under water. Among other things, they regularly feed on fish. In addition, they have a curious streak that is famous among outdoorsmen. They have been known to drop into the boat with anglers, and they will swim right up to a float tube.

Had I spooked the snake? Was it headed for a more private spot to continue its morning sunbathing, or had I sparked its interest enough to warrant coming over to check me out? Would my bare legs be strange enough to cause it to turn away, or would it be inspired to give them a snaky lick?

I guarded myself against panic should I feel its cool body intertwining with my legs. An uncertain or sudden move on my part would mean instant injection, an interminable crawl back to the car, and a miserable several days.

Worry. Anxiety. Fretting. The Bible explicitly instructs us to avoid these enemies. "Be anxious for nothing," Paul writes in Philippians 4:6. "Do not worry," Jesus teaches in Matthew 6:31. "Do not fret," David says in Psalm 37:8. As I consider these admonitions I can't help but wonder if any of them were ever thigh deep in a muddy river with a poisonous snake (see Acts 28:3).

Worry is assuming responsibility for something that is God's responsibility. God is explicit about carrying burdens that are not ours to tote. Yet I find myself laboring under loads I was never designed to carry. Is it any wonder I struggle and ache inside when I stress myself beyond my maker's design?

God inspired David to state imperatively, "Cast your burden upon the LORD" (Ps. 55:22). Our heavenly Father promises that his burdens are light in Matthew 11:30. Paul goes on to write in Philippians 4:6–7 that we are to pray about everything, and the peace of God, which surpasses all comprehension, will guard our hearts and our minds.

It has been my experience that letting God have what is his to carry is easier said than done. It is as if I believe massaging and manipulating the stress that plagues me is a noble calling, a duty I must fulfill in order to be diligent.

Just last night I lay awake in my Rochester, Minnesota, hotel room tossing and turning, and I don't just mean on the bed. I tossed and turned four phone calls over and over as if I were flipping coins to make a decision. I also tossed between giving my burdens to Father and then turning them back toward me. I'm not sure if I ultimately won or just wore out. All I know is the clock read single digits the last time I looked.

The stout, gray moccasin served a valuable purpose. I forgot about the snake after several minutes, but I continued to consider the nature of worry. When it comes down to it, I must decide if I am going to let God carry his responsibilities or if I am going to carry them for him and be guilty of worry.

## Something to Consider

Are you prone to worry? How about fret? Do you experience just a little anxiety every now and then?

If you truly believe God will take care of you, why do you insist on worrying? Worry assumes God can't—or won't—take care of you, and that is simply not true!

What do you hope to gain by gambling with worry? "What do you mean by 'gambling'?" you ask. When we attempt to carry a load specifically designed to be carried by God, we are gambling that we will be able to carry something intended for him. The gamble is that you will either be successful and get to pretend that you can do what God does or be broken by a load too heavy for you to carry.

The point, however, is not whether or not to gamble. The point is that either way, you lose. You were never intended to carry God's burdens, and independence from God is not a virtue. It is always sin.

Why not review the four-step process from the last chapter, relinquish the tendency you have to worry and fret, and fling your ungracious burden of worry in God's direction? He will take what you cast off.

## MEDITATION
### & RESPONSE

*Father, I don't want to delude myself, and I know better than to try to fool you. The boundaries between planning, thoughtful consideration, and worry are fuzzy in my mind.*

*I know I am to be diligent. I realize I am to be wise. It is clear that I must plan and project and trust that you will give me insight beyond my innate abilities. And I know from experience the revelations and insights related to these necessary and appropriate exercises often come late in the night after hours of work and frustration. This I know to be reality.*

*What is the difference between diligence and worry?*

*Papa, correct me if I'm wrong, but I think the difference between thoughtful planning and worry is my confidence level in your sufficiency. If this is so, then make me sensitive to my attitudes of independence. Help me to recognize the enemy's accusation that you are not sufficient. And give me the courageous resolve to grasp your grace in the ungracious place of looming worry.*

*Thanks, Papa.*

# thirteen

# Fear

How are you doing managing your fears? Ignoring them or denying their existence doesn't count as a management style. They are still there whether you acknowledge them or are aware of them. Saying you don't struggle with fears because you deny their existence in your life is like saying the sun didn't come up because you have your hands over your eyes.

Fear assumes the absence of God. Fear is the belief that God either isn't there for you or that you are capable apart from God based upon your inventory of personal resources. Walking after the flesh is synonymous with walking in fear. If walking after the flesh is living independently of God, then it is what you do when you play God instead of letting God be God in your life. Flesh, like fear, is the absence of God. I was reminded recently that the first thing Adam said to God after he and Eve declared independence and sinned was "I was afraid." It is noteworthy that the first thing God said when Christ was born was "Fear not" (Luke 2:10 KJV).

In simple terms, the struggle in our lives is between independence and dependence, fear and love, flesh and spirit, self-sufficiency and reliance upon Father. When we live independently, we are controlled by our fears. Walking in the Spirit, depending upon our heavenly Father, is living beyond our fears in perfect love, and the Bible says, "Perfect love casts out fear" (1 John 4:18).

To define fear as the physiological reaction you have when you barely miss a car wreck is too narrow. Adding the intangible and hypothetical anxiety you experience still doesn't create a definition that encompasses fear's reaches.

If fear is the absence of God, then all you do in response to God's absence constitutes fear. Your self-confidence, your quest for competency, your determination to be a wise manager of your finances, your effort to do the right thing, and your care for those around you can all be encompassed in fear. If these efforts—no matter how praiseworthy—have been crafted to control your environment, gain acceptance for yourself, maintain your lifestyle, and please others, then they are fear and flesh because God is not your source.

Depending upon your heavenly Father is living in perfect love, and perfect love casts out fear. In other words, either you place God in control or you live in fear. There are only two choices before you: You can live in fear or you can live in perfect love. You can walk after the flesh or you can walk in the Spirit. You can live legalistically or you can find your resource in grace. I have said the same thing several different ways, but fundamentally, these are our only two choices.

So when I ask how you are doing at managing your fears, I'm asking how you are doing at walking in the Spirit, how you are doing living in perfect love, how you are doing thriving in grace, how you are doing residing in Christ's sufficiency, how you are doing basking in Father's love.

When you get right down to it, at the heart of every fear is the presupposition that God is not present, not in control, and not sufficient. This is a contradiction of who God is and how he designed you to live. You are no more designed to live in flesh and fear than Adam was, and your heavenly Father has made provision for the fears that plague you. He announced his plan through the angels on the night of Christ's incarnation in Bethlehem's manger: "Fear not!" Jesus echoed his Father's declaration when he said to his disciples, "Take courage, it is I; do not be afraid." He went on to promise, "I will never leave you." And if perfect love casts out fear, as the Bible asserts, then John sums it all up for us when he says, "God is love," and "God so loved."

My dear friend, our challenge is clear: If we cling to our fears, we declare to ourselves and all who observe our lives that God is neither sufficient nor worthy. We must live in perfect love and let perfect love be reflected in our lives. This is the only real choice we have as people whose hearts desire to please Father. This is the only real choice that will bring freedom from fear.

Whether your fears are for today, tomorrow, your kids, your job, your emotional strength, your mental well-being, spiritual courage, the acceptance of others, war, or loss, "perfect love casts out fear." Living in Christ is the only way to manage fear. Living in Christ's strength is the only option other than the flesh.

## Something to Consider

I live with chronic pain, and it has escalated in intensity the last few months. One thing about discomfort is that Satan never misses an opportunity to instill fear. Dread, distress, and anxiety knock on my door daily, delivering messages from the enemy sealed in an envelope of fear.

What does my future hold? If I feel this way now, what will my condition be when I'm fifty or sixty? I was holding my own against this foe, but I'm losing ground fast. When will I be able to stem the losses I'm suffering? Will I ever ride my bicycle again? What if I can't recover my lost ground?

This is one of my ungracious places and a little insight into the fears it engenders. But God is sufficient—even at this writing, with pain screaming for attention. If I listen closely—and I must to hear over the cacophony of pain—I hear Father saying, "Do not be afraid. I am with you."

So I challenge you to consider this: What are your fears, and how are you doing at managing them?

## MEDITATION
### & RESPONSE

*Father, fear has me surrounded. There is not a day, not even a moment, that I don't hurt. And knowing pain intimately and seeing its face constantly, I am still tempted to run the race on my own. Sometimes—no, often-times—it is as though it never occurs to me to cast my cares and my pains and my fear onto you. No wonder I am surrounded by fear!*

*Father, I thank you for your love. I thank you for concluding it wasn't enough to say you loved me. Thank you for resolving in your heart to demonstrate your love by joining me*

*in the battle and promising that you would
never leave me to fight alone.*

*One of these days I will enjoy the comfort
of your embrace. But right now, I relish the
comfort of your warrior spirit. I treasure the
camaraderie of our battles together and the
memories we share of great campaigns we
have launched against the enemy.*

*I deeply appreciate the familial love you
readily convey to me, but I also thank you for
the brotherly love you have planted in my
heart, the affection of best friends, and the
confidence that is mine as your blessed son.
You have taught me what you know of fear,
the enemy, who you are, and who I am.*

*You are my mentor, my Father, my older
brother, my friend. I call upon the grace of
your love to cast out fear in the ungracious
places of my life.*

*Thanks, Papa.*

fourteen

# Threat

I awoke at 4:03 A.M. to the sound of a police helicopter. Turns out there was a burglar a few streets over making his second attempt at forcible entry in ten days. Police cruisers patrolled the streets, and the helicopter hovered over the neighborhood for half an hour. The only one in our house who slept through the whole affair was the dog, which I don't understand. I thought we had the dog for occasions such as this, so our minds would be at ease and Dianne and I could sleep securely.

Standard routine at our house has the alarm clock sound at 5:00 A.M., followed by one touch of the snooze. Then it is showers, breakfast, a few quiet moments, stretching, and a workout, in varying order depending on the day of the week and whether it is Di's schedule or mine. The only critical constant is for the shower to follow the workout.

But today we both piled out with the alarm's first declaration of morning—no sense lying in bed any longer. All except for the dog, that is. She doesn't pay any more attention to the morning alarm than she does to helicopters or burglars three streets over.

I stretched out to loosen up my cantankerous back and retreated to my chair in the TV room, threw a comforter over my lap, and opened to the third Proverb. "My son, do not forget my teaching," it began.

Even though I had spent the last hour of my sleep time listening for the ominous sounds of a burglar outside our house, my mind was primarily focused on yesterday. As the children's book would describe it, it had been a terrible, horrible, no good, very bad day. I had been impugned and slighted. My feelings had been hurt rather profoundly—and not for the first time—by a colleague and friend in another city.

I sat for a moment or two with my Bible in my lap wondering why the unpleasant event of yesterday had transpired and what I should do about it, but I was no closer to understanding it or knowing what to do now than I had been after I hung up the phone fifteen hours earlier. So I looked down and read further. "Do not let kindness and truth leave you; bind them around your neck, write them on the tablet of your heart. . . . Trust in the LORD with all your heart and do not lean on your own understanding. In all your ways acknowledge Him, and He will make your paths straight" (vv. 3–6).

First, I gained perspective about my standard: While still unclear about what to do, I realized I must never digress from kindness and truth, no matter how profound the ungraciousness foisted upon me. Based upon the text, this is easier said than done; otherwise, why would it say "bind" and "write"?

Second, I was reminded that I must trust Father and not depend on my own smarts. Regardless of what course of action I decide to take, I must acknowledge Christ as my life.

And finally, I realized God would make my path straight. I like that. I'm the type that likes to get on with it once a goal is established or a destination is declared. No messing around. Straight is a good thing.

But by the same token, nowhere does the text imply that straight is synonymous with easy or expeditious. Curvy roads are curvy because they avoid the more challenging, more costly, more demanding route. It is no mystery why you don't encounter straight paths very often. Straight doesn't go around. Straight goes up, down, through, and over. Curves accommodate. Straight considers the ungraciousness that lies ahead and charts a gracious course that is the most direct route to the other side. Straight considers the destination and resources in inventory rather than the slop and stench of the ungracious course ahead. The straight path showcases the grandeur of grace against the backdrop of ungracious places.

As though offering encouragement for the day, the chapter went ahead to say, "Do not be afraid of sudden fear nor of the onslaught of the wicked when it comes; for the LORD will be your confidence and will keep your foot from being caught" (vv. 25–26). Now those are good words for hurt feelings, as well as uncertain feelings about the burglar lurking in the neighborhood.

The police tell me they failed to apprehend the burglar. If the status quo remains intact, I'll hear the helicopter again in the night, the dog will remain curled up on her bed, and I'll get another chance to review the grace of Proverbs 3 in the ungracious place of lost sleep.

While I have no hope of explaining the significance of the helicopter to the dog, in hopes that she will assume the responsibility of protecting us from this robber, I do have a choice about traveling a curvy road or a straight one. Straight is a good thing.

## Something to Consider

When I consider the straight path, as opposed to the curvy path, I think of keeping my eyes focused on Jesus, "the author and perfecter of faith." Hebrews 12:2 describes the nature of the course and Jesus' decision to choose the course he did instead of the other options available to him: "who for the joy set before Him endured the cross, despising the shame, and has sat down at the right hand of the throne of God."

Almost as if on cue, Father charts the course he has in mind for us and the means by which we are to navigate the terrain. Verse 3 reads, "For consider Him who has endured such hostility by sinners against Himself, so that you will not grow weary and lose heart."

Let me illustrate the straight course with this: In a church where I was a member, there was a flamboyant attorney who had an ego the size of Texas, a mouth the size of Alaska, and the tact of a bull in a china closet. He chewed perpetually on a foot-long cigar, wore a diamond tie tack the size of a peach pit, dressed in white suits with alligator boots and a Panama hat, and had a loudspeaker behind the grill of his Continental that he used to announce his arrival at social functions—like church—and speak to his friends as he drove down the street.

Though certainly not by choice, I tangled with him a time or two. He used his power and position as an ugly, humiliating, and downright inhumane club to bolster his ever-ravenous ego.

I have taken this opportunity to introduce you to this fellow because his wife's name was Grace, and she was his antithesis. In addition to being absolutely lovely in appearance, even in her old age, she was kind, beneficent, congenial, and everything else her husband was not.

Grace was my personification of grace. Mention grace to me, I thought of Grace. But when I thought of her, I thought of her self-effacing, accommodating, unflappable class in stark contrast to her roguish, ungracious husband. It wasn't until I got a bit older and understood some of the resolve it takes to live with someone in marriage that I garnered a different insight into the determination of grace by considering Grace.

Grace could have chosen nearly any course she wished in our small town. She could have had her husband done in and buried in a shallow grave, taken his seat on the judge's bench without an election, and never been questioned or blamed. I used to wonder why Grace didn't do this. If she weren't gone, I would like to ask her if it wasn't because she opted for the straight course instead of the expedient options available to her. She was an amazing woman. Upon reflection, I can't imagine what it took for Grace to live with her husband.

But then again, I think I can imagine. Grace in ungracious places is something we can all identify with. I am more inspired that grace goes through un-grace on the straight course, mirroring many of the character qualities exemplified by Grace.

What does the straight course of grace look like in the ungracious place where you stand?

Have you noticed that the straight path is sometimes the harder course and that what is best for you is often what appears to be the most ungracious?

When standing in the sloppy mess of an ungracious place, should you cut your losses, opt for the curving path, and assume the accommodations are grace with a different face?

## MEDITATION & RESPONSE

*Father, I choose grace, and I discard decisively any notion of grace as a weak, Sunday only, milquetoast matter of theology and declare grace the courageous declaration of your invasion of my life. I want to meet my daily life in the same way you did.*

*Father, thank you for bringing all that you are to the ungracious task of rescuing me from my independence, sin, arrogance, and separation from you. Thank you for listening to my feeble cry for deliverance, and in response to that slight invitation, seizing the opportunity to invade hell, rescue me, and make me your own. But most of all, thank you for taking the straight path to get to me.*

*Father, I want to exemplify your grace in my ungracious places like you demonstrated your grace to me. Father, would you do this through me? Would you let me share the glory of your life by living a life of grace in this ungracious place?*

*Thanks, Papa.*

# fifteen

# Embarrassment

Have you ever done something so stupid that you totally embarrassed yourself and left no hope of reclaiming your lost dignity? Yeah, me too.

I could feel the warmth of the blood running inside my nose as my eyes clouded over with tears. I looked around, taking a quick inventory of any potential witnesses, nodded to an approaching woman, and then reached up to touch my nose. Blood was making its precipitous trek down my face and mouth in rivulets.

I bent over instinctively to protect my dress shirt and began making my way for a grassy patch vaguely visible through the glassy fog. I held my nose and squeezed it back into place. The blood was coming quickly now.

Five minutes earlier I stepped from my office to go to the men's room only to discover that the security officer was locking the door. A main water valve thingamajig that serviced all of the men's rooms in our office tower had given up on life. "You'll have to go to Tower One and use the rest room on the first floor," the security officer said.

Down the hall, left to the elevator, ride five floors, weave through the lobby, past the auditorium, out the double glass doors, across the breezeway, through another set of double glass doors, and into the lobby of the adjacent tower. I looked right; I looked left. I wandered here; I wandered there. I passed the cafeteria. I thought about asking for directions but then came to my senses. "I'm a man. I can't ask for directions," I muttered. Ah, a clue: the water fountain. Sure enough. Finally.

With that taken care of and the course plotted for my return trip to the office, my mind returned to the work I had been focused on moments earlier. Remember those double glass doors I passed through coming into Tower One? While I was in the men's room someone propped the outer door open, which I noticed immediately. However, I forgot all about the inside door.

I never saw it coming. My head was turned slightly to the left and I was walking briskly, full speed actually, as I was late for staff meeting. I heard the noise before I felt anything and wondered for a moment whether my abrupt stop caused the noise or was in response to the noise. In light of the rapidly escalating pain, I deduced that the former was the case.

While my head buzzed, my nose and forehead began complaining vociferously. This concerned me, but my first priority was clear: *I wonder who witnessed this stupid move. How can I adequately explain why I just walked into a door I have passed through a dozen times? I have shattered any dignity and composure I ordinarily exude.*

Mercifully, there was just the one woman approaching the Tower One lobby, and I didn't recognize her. I quickly nodded from a distance, ducked my head, and diverted my course for the grass.

Once it became evident that this was no small problem, I made my way back inside to the men's room, trying my best to calculate the direct route that had evaded me moments earlier. Examination in the mirror revealed a cut on the bridge of my nose, a blue welt just off center between my eyebrows, and the persistent bleeding coming from inside my swelling, darkening schnozzle.

My nose seemed relatively straight when lined up with the tiles on the wall of the men's room, although it did need a bit more adjustment from my preliminary work outside, and air seemed to be passing on both sides. *But what in the world am I going to tell the staff? I'm already late for the staff meeting. If it weren't for the cut and that growing blue mound, they would never have to know about this incessant buzzing in my head and tightening in my face. I guess I'll have to be honest about what happened.*

That last thought caught my attention. *Why would I not be honest? Here I am, broken and bleeding, and the devil is tempting me to lie. But, I'll admit, it would make matters considerably less embarrassing if I could think up a reasonable alibi.* And then, another thought, from the other side of the arena: *I wonder if my identity in Christ applies to this dilemma?* I took that thought to be from the Holy Spirit.

You know the answer as well as I do. Of course it applies. Father didn't call us "accepted" and "secure" so that we could announce it while cruising the streets of heaven. These facts will be self-evident up there. It is here, on this earth, that I need the confidence of nonnegotiable, immovable, unbending acceptance and security. And it was during the three-minute walk back to the office that I needed to practice setting my mind on this fact, which is exactly what I did.

As you might suspect, I was late getting to the staff meeting. I took my seat at the head of the conference table and launched into my story about being accosted by hoodlums who took my money and landed one blow to my nose before I successfully fought them off, saved a woman and her child whom they had kidnapped, called the police, and . . . and then I laughed and told them the truth.

What a great reminder. We know Father makes provision for the major crises in life, but he works the details just as hard. Just like the friend he is, while I was occupied with keeping the blood off of my shirt and trying to get my nose straightened out, he was encouraging me that I was accepted and secure with him, and he had seen me walk into the door. Not even that changed his mind about me.

## Something to Consider

The theology we create, trying to wrap our arms around an infinite, all-knowing, all-powerful God who loves us in spite of our unworthiness, is often so high and heavenly minded it is of little earthly good. Big words get thrown around: eschatology, hermeneutics, ecclesiology, epistemology.

What I want to know—need desperately to know—is whether I'm secure in the men's room. How about you? Is your faith real to you? Is your relationship with God characterized by theological information or the pragmatic, everyday reality of friendship?

Over the course of my spiritual experience, there have been those who tried to create spiritual hunger and growth with questions like these: Are you prepared to die for your faith? If they were ready to turn the lions loose on you, would you still claim the name of Christ? If they came and took all your Bibles from you, would you have enough Scripture memorized to feed your soul?

Those are good questions, but what I really want to know is, am I secure in the men's room? When I am embarrassed because of something stupid I did, am I secure in my identity? When my self-esteem is shot full of holes, and I pulled the trigger, am I still accepted? How about you?

# MEDITATION
## & RESPONSE

*Father, I know all of the heady things and deep truths of your Word are important. But when I prioritize the issues in my life, I don't think I can devote the time and attention necessary to build the superstructure of my faith when the foundation is cracked and I'm uncertain about its viability.*

*It is one thing to give you the successes. It is one thing to credit you for a staff meeting conducted in stellar style. It is one thing to honor you with a speech that holds the audience spellbound. But it is another to give you my broken nose, ask you to help me keep the blood off my good shirt, and clear my eyes so I can see the tiles well enough to reset my nose and get it straight.*

*But Father, I give you my moments of grace and un-grace, recognizing that your grace is pervasive. I ask that you would take the glorious moments as well as the ignominious failures, and by your grace turn both into living reflections of your heart.*

*Thanks, Papa.*

# Grace in
# Ugly Places

sixteen

# Attack

W here were you on September 11, 2001, when terrorists attacked America? I was sitting at my desk, working diligently on this book. Someone from my office called and asked if I was watching the news. I got up from my computer and turned on the television just in time to see the aftermath of the second plane crash.

What an incredible, horrific turn our lives took on that Tuesday morning! Adequately capturing the magnitude of suffering, grief, and fury is still mind-numbingly frustrating. Why should our language—or anyone's—be asked to provide expression for something so horrific? Perhaps by comparing these atrocities to the tragic chain of events at Pearl Harbor sixty years ago, we find a modicum of expression in President Roosevelt's words, "Today is a day that will live in infamy." Indeed, September 11, 2001, lives in infamy.

There is the dawning, stark realization in all of us that before this nightmare is over, all of us are destined to feel grief's grip in profound and personal ways. None of us can escape this trauma or the fallout that follows. The suffering is worldwide.

The depths of this present and impending darkness are virtually unknown in our lifetime. It is as though we are looking the devil in the face and being summoned to his lair. Ungracious concoctions bubble in the caldron of our souls. Fear, rage, revenge, sorrow, disbelief, embarrassment, and profane words we have not used in years—or perhaps that have never passed the portcullis of our teeth—now escape our lips.

When we begin to sort through the rubble of our way of life, our national pride, our skylines, and our immense human loss, I think the question becomes, where was God on September 11, 2001?

God is on his throne, and this is a true and accurate fact. He is not aloof! He is present, and he is not silent. The Holy Spirit is not absent but in us, and he prays on our behalf when we don't have the words we need to convey what is on our minds and in our hearts. Jesus Christ faced the devil eye to eye at the darkest moment in history, and he did so alone. He is in us to face whatever befalls us. We are not alone, and God is not absent.

Make no mistake, in these days of infamy, God is not only sufficient, he is more than enough. Jesus Christ is the same today as he was yesterday and will be tomorrow. And the Holy Spirit, the Comforter, the One Called Alongside to Help, our Helper, lives in us as a constant reminder of Christ's pledge, "I will not leave you as orphans" (John 14:18).

We have not seen the end of this tragedy. In fact, I'm afraid we have not even seen the beginning of the end.

The road before us is treacherous, and it is heartrending. The pain of this journey will be, as former Mayor Giuliani of New York City said, "more than any of us can bear."

Shouting above the din of anguish, I hear Father's instructions to us, "Cast [literally, "fling"] your burden upon the LORD" (Ps. 55:22). Listen to his counsel! This is not theological instruction for you to consider the next time you get a chance to go to Sunday school. Father is pleading with us, offering advice essential to our well-being: Fling the burdens tumbling onto you in his direction.

This bears no resemblance to hanging up your freshly pressed shirts for the closet rod to bear. This is a furious, desperate, flinging aside of that debris choking your soul and burying your spirit. Father's words are not pleasant, placid suggestions taken from a pretty picture on a wall calendar. These are words of instruction from One who has been to hell and back and lived to tell about it.

In the meantime, through the cacophony of this infamy, our heavenly Father is not silent. He is shouting to us from all directions. Listen for his voice.

Do not be deceived. Our lives will be reduced to the fundamentals in relatively short order. Life will take on a blunt, determined resolve of will. Much of what we think of as the grace and ease of life will disappear. But make no mistake. Grace has not been lost. He is in you, around you, before you, behind you, and expressing his life through you—even in the ungraciousness of your terror and fury. Watch for him. Follow his lead. Take his counsel and fling your concerns upon him.

## Something to Consider

I have referenced the Scripture that says we are to fling our burdens in God's direction. And how often will you have to cast what concerns you onto God? Repeatedly.

Frequently. In succession. Oftentimes, you will have to cast intense burdens on him continually.

The enemy will be quick to ask the question, "Why do you continue this exercise in futility? If God was capable of carrying your load he would have taken it by now. I don't believe he is anywhere to be found!"

Baloney!

On the contrary. In the un-grace of these days, there is plenty of anguish and heaviness to go around. The devil does not lack for concerns to load on your back, and just as soon as you clear out a space, he will dump a fresh bucket of his ungraciousness on top of you.

You must not give up even though you are tired of the fight. The scenario we are living through in these days is akin to bailing water out of a boat during a ferocious storm. Take the things that weigh you down and fling them in Father's direction. And be a realist during these days, not a spiritualist. You will have to do this with res-olute determination on a frequent basis, not because Father fails to take what you give him, but because the devil loads you down in hopes of breaking your will to trust Father.

Consider this: The Pentagon and World Trade Center were not the only sites attacked by terrorists. You are under attack as well!

## MEDITATION
### & RESPONSE

*Father, it is hard for me to comprehend the tragic turn of events of September 11. Under-standing the destruction, death, and war that resulted is just beyond my grasp. And the seri-*

*ous nature of Satan's terror in my life is almost surreal. I want to wake up from the nightmare of the devil's ungraciousness in my life.*

*Father, I have no better words to pray now than I did in September. Holy Spirit, I ask you to pray and intercede on my behalf. Please guide me, direct me into your wisdom, and help me discern your voice amidst all the hollering inside this whirlwind.*

*You say you give grace to the afflicted, and that you do. I could wish for deliverance, but I am thrilled with your grace. I have an opportunity to see you shine as never before. And given that thought, I ask that you shine your light through me. Let me be a representative of grace in ungracious places.*

*Thanks, Papa.*

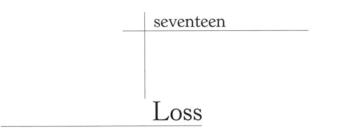

seventeen

# Loss

First Samuel 30 is not recommended reading for children under twelve or adults with squeamish stomachs. Fire, war, plunder, slaughter, stoning, starvation, and general inhumanity are just some of the reasons this chapter isn't on the good-for-before-bedtime reading list.

Dianne likes reading about Ruth and Boaz falling in love, Miriam rescuing baby Moses, and Esther winning the Miss Media-Persia beauty contest to become queen. But chapter 30 is my kind of passage: men escaping mayhem, riding camels across the desert, dividing the spoils of war. I tried using these verses for our evening devotional a few nights ago, but Dianne said we should go back

to our devotional guide as soon as possible, preferably yesterday—something about it being a "man thing."

I'm being facetious, but only about the part regarding
Dianne. It's not hard to see how some of David's most
meaningful psalms were penned during the days described
in chapter 30. David's hometown had been plundered by
marauders, and everything was gone: wives, children, live-
stock, possessions. The city had been burned to the ground,
and the men in David's army spoke of stoning him because
of their bitter loss and anguished souls.

Had you been in David's shoes, what would you have
done?

He had several options: gather up the men ready to stone
him and show them a thing or two; take a loyalty poll and
decide whether to abdicate or fight; give up and say, "I quit";
blame someone else; or put the troops in formation and
march off to get even. Any of these seem reasonable given
the circumstances and the distress he was feeling.

But David's reaction was extraordinary: Samuel writes
that "David strengthened himself in the LORD his God"
(v. 6) and then, calmly and methodically, asked the Lord
what he had in mind for him to do. Only then did he round
up his grieving troops and pursue the Amalekites who had
perpetrated this atrocious evil.

How did David strengthen himself in the Lord? Can we
follow suit?

David sits alone on the rubble of what was once his
home. His heart spasms with despair, and he longs to hear
the ecstatic greeting of his family gathering around him.
He's home from his trip and all has gone well, but they are
. . . who knows where, perhaps dead.

The silence is eerie. It harbors grieving men and bitter
souls alone with their thoughts. Like David, they had hopes
and anticipation for arriving home. They hadn't been expected back so soon, so each had been thinking, *What fun
it will be to watch the kids' jaws drop in astonishment when I*

*walk through the door. I should make it just in time for dinner. My wife will wrap her arms around my neck. They'll think I'm a dream come true.*

*Nightmare* is a more apt description of the reality that lies smoking in the valley as David and his army gaze from the hill outside town at what was once home. Each man labors under the weight of his own burden—except for David. In addition to his own pain, he is yoked to the grief of every man, woman, and child under his care. Alone with the weight of the world, the fire illuminates his warrior face. No one sees his tears except God, and he catches each drop (ref. Ps. 56:8).

Deep inside, far into the recesses of the man where spirit and soul become indistinguishable, David contemplates what he knows, and there he begins to take issue against the enemy's counsel. *It would be sheer folly to depend upon the resources of my army to attack this problem. The Lord doesn't need the strength of my horses or the numbers of my men. God is my refuge and strength, a very present help in trouble and in the day of my distress. I will sing of his strength and joyfully sing of his lovingkindness. My flesh and my heart may fail; but God is the strength of my heart and my portion forever. I will seek the Lord and his strength and determine to do so continually. The Lord is my strength and song. The Lord is my shield; my heart trusts him, and I am helped; therefore my heart exults, and with my song I shall thank him* (paraphrased from Ps. 33:17; 46:1; 59:16; 73:26; 105:4; 118:14; 147:10; 28:7).

David thanks the Lord and his heart exults, but not like the devil would like for you to think. David does not come to the conclusion that God is still on his throne, resolve to trust him, and begin dancing on the rubble of his burned estate. Psalm 47:1, "Clap your hands, all peoples; shout to God with the voice of joy," was not penned at this moment. I doubt seriously that you would have heard any melodious, toe-tapping sounds emanating from the songwriter soon to be king.

The intention of his heart and the song of his soul were being measured out deliberately, deep within the inner man. If composed, the score for these words would read *"Andante* with fortitude." These weren't dance tunes. They were steady, major chords of resolute encouragement. Not flowery lyrics but simple words of truth and affirmation fueled the spiritual boiler within David's heart.

Beside the smoldering remains, alone, through tears, with assassination plots festering in the dark, a deliberate counterforce begins to take issue with the onslaught of the enemy. With mounting determination, a spiritual tug-of-war begins. The momentum of the enemy and his contingent degenerates into an apparent stalemate with the hosts of heaven. And then, ever so slowly, like a locomotive turning the wheels of a loaded freight train, the strength of the Lord begins the process of reclaiming lost ground.

Like a fighter David doesn't bolt and run or sidestep the pain. He faces the challenge before him, stays in the ring, and wades into the fray. How else would he be able to write the words we read above and take issue against the enemy's counsel? For every conundrum constructed by the enemy, David counters with confidence anchored in truth.

Picture it: The Bible says *all* the people were bitter and spoke of stoning David. Had I been in his sandals, I think my first words would have been, "Okay. Everybody put your rocks down and let's talk reasonably about this predicament." But not this man! David has been chased all over creation by Saul, dodging spears and hiding out in the wilderness. If asked, I think he would say, "When the Lord takes me home it will be because he's ready, not because a bunch of angry guys decide to stone me." I don't think it ever crossed his mind to ask his men to put down their rocks.

I hear only the strength and confidence of the Lord when David says to Abiathar, the priest, "Please bring me the ephod." (The ephod was used in those days for praying.) A fearful, insecure man would not say "Please." That simple word tells us the internal peace of God was being expressed through David.

With dignity and confidence, he faced the mounting hardship. In other words, David wasn't strengthened because the Lord told him that he would recover all that had been lost (1 Sam. 30:8). He was strengthened before he ever asked for the ephod. If the people stoned him, he was strengthened. If he never saw his family again, he was strengthened. If Abiathar refused to bring him the ephod, he was strengthened. He was strengthened even as he sat on the ashes of his home.

Being strengthened in the Lord doesn't mean your emotions change or the circumstances change, but it does mean your confidence in the Lord surges and the locomotive of the Spirit begins to build spiritual momentum.

So sit down right where you are. Your perch may be a charred remnant, a pile of rubble that used to be a home, the front seat of your pickup, the kitchen table, or your mahogany and leather desk chair. But sit down. Let's strengthen ourselves in the Lord. Personalize these thoughts along with me:

> It would be sheer folly to depend upon my resources to attack the issues before me. The gifts, power, influence, and strength available to me are a false hope for victory. God is my refuge and strength. He dwells inside me in the form of the Holy Spirit and has been my stronghold and refuge when I have been distressed. Why wouldn't he be the same today? My flesh and my heart may fail, but God is the strength of my heart now and throughout all time. I will seek the Lord and his strength and determine to do so continually. The Lord is my strength, my shield, and my song. I trust him. And just by doing so, I am helped (paraphrased from Ps. 33:17; 46:1; 59:16; 73:26; 105:4; 118:14; 147:10; 28:7).

Stand up. Spread your arms open wide. Gaze toward Father and take a deep breath. With that breath, step into the light of his grace in this ungracious place and utter this resolve: "Thank you, Father. Grace is my choice today. Now I have decisions to make, a mess to clean up, people to work with, and a few fires to put out. I realize you don't need reminding, but I do. As I stand up to deal with these issues, I'm depending on your strength."

## Something to Consider

It is not often we have the privilege of reading someone's journal. Such writings are far too personal. But such is not the case with David. The Psalms are his journal, the Books of Samuel are his memoirs, and in a candid revelation of this man's failures, I find the courage to examine the journal of my own life and look for Father's fingerprints: grace in ungracious places.

As you consider the journal of your life, where do Father's fingerprints appear most frequently?

## MEDITATION & RESPONSE

*Father, I know you are a God of miracles. You drowned the Egyptian army in the Red Sea, sent the fish to soften Jonah so he would listen to you, raised Lazarus, and defeated the grave. I am impressed and awed.*

*But for all the glory of your miraculous adventures, I thank you for your grace. Like David, I identify with the building momentum* of the Spirit's locomotive within my soul. I want to stoke that fire. I want to build a spiritual head of steam that powers me forward.

I know your grace and the bond between us fuels this furnace within my heart. Pour on the fuel! My heart's desire is to be strengthened in the power of your might and the strength of your Word.

Thanks, Papa.

eighteen

# Injustice

Matthew 14:1–12 recounts the death—execution actually—of John the Baptist. This man was not only the greatest of the prophets, but according to his cousin, Jesus, there has never been a man as great as John. He was chosen to pave the way for the Messiah. Said another way, he was given the task of going before God on his venture into humanity.

John did a great job. He baptized Jesus. He was loyal to his calling. He lived a holy life. He took a Nazarite vow of holiness and kept it. He mentored his disciples. He did not compromise in order to gain notoriety, popularity, or acceptance. John was a good man—on second thought, John was a great man.

And how is it that God permits John to be removed from the scene so the Messiah can flourish? What sort of exit does John, the forbearer of Christ, make from life? How is the greatest man who has ever lived, apart from Christ himself, taken to his eternal reward? He dies early in life, perhaps leaving grieving parents. He dies unjustly, as face-saving payment on a foolish oath inspired by a lurid, sensuous dance during a drunken feast.

Salome, a young woman, comes in and dances for King Herod, his military leaders, cabinet personnel, and civic potentates. I can't imagine, nor do any of the commentators report, anything other than a suggestive, luring, sexually stimulating striptease, otherwise why would Herod and his guests be so pleased in their morally and mentally compromised state?

Prompted by Herodias, her mother and Herod's sister-in-law and bed partner, Salome asks for John's head on a platter. To save face with his friends, Herod has John beheaded, and no doubt watches—intoxicated with wine and lust—Salome dance again, in some state of undress, with John's head on a silver platter running over with blood and drool.

The greatest man of all time reaches his end without a trial, sentencing, final words, witnesses, or even a demonstration by his followers. His head is paraded on a plate in front of a drunken party of the rich and famous in a pornographic dance.

John the Baptist served God, loved God, and honored God more than any before or after, and his exit is more horrendous and ignominious than any mentioned at the conclusion of Hebrews 11—which tells of martyrs who died horrific deaths—or the balance of Scripture. His was not even a martyr's death. He was killed over the foolish, drunken oath of an insecure, lustful, power-hungry man who wanted to save face among his equally inebriated friends and subjects.

As I consider John's death and the ungracious nature of his exit from this life and consider the expectations I place on God and the entitlement I feel is due me for my service and loyalty to the kingdom—whether this be the standard of living I enjoy, the friends I keep, or the death I die—I must question the nature of my expectations. Certainly they set me up for disappointment, as do all expectations, but this is only the minimum projected loss. On a greater scale, my expectations for this life also indicate a false, shallow anticipation of something better in this life because of my service and loyalty to God. Restated, my expectations harbor the belief that I will be rewarded with something of heaven on earth for having done deeds that elicit God's favor. How shortsighted!

Life is not about me and what is best for me. My life, like John's, is about pointing the way to Father. It is about loving and enjoying God. It is about perpetually developing the theme and plot of the true fairy tale in which God is the hero. To illustrate this point, let's consider a popular fairy tale.

In "Sleeping Beauty," the princess and the entire kingdom sleep for a hundred years under the spell of the wicked fairy. For a century, brave knights and noblemen attempt to hack their way through the briar forest surrounding the castle to rescue the sleeping beauty.

The hero of the story, a handsome prince, rides up to the briar forest and hears the legend of the sleeping princess. He listens to the dread stories of death, all along contemplating a daring rescue attempt of his own. As he considers the challenge, a hundred years' worth of dead men's bones lay entangled in the briar forest, attesting to their torturous deaths and the impossibility of making it through the thorns. It doesn't look good for Sleeping Beauty.

But the hero of the story, with great courage and resolve, draws his sword—a sword of light, the fairy tale reads—and hacks his way through the briar forest and its man-killing thorns. He slays the wicked fairy, who has disguised herself as a fire-breathing dragon, and searches for the sleeping

133

princess until he finds her in a portion of the castle so remote not even her father, the king, knew it existed. He kisses her, she awakens—and the entire kingdom with her—and they all live happily ever after.

What a marvelous story of honor, bravery, and redemption. But the story is enhanced, and the hero elevated to heroic proportion, by the thorns, the forest, the dragon, the curse, the knights' search for Sleeping Beauty, and the kiss. Only one warrior prevailed over all obstacles, made it to the castle, and rescued the fair maiden. All the others served to make the accomplishment of the one brave warrior that much more profound and noteworthy.

I'm not advocating that we canonize "Sleeping Beauty." But sometimes it helps to have a different perspective in order to arrive at a fresh point of view. God uses metaphors and similes all the time in his Word—bride, groom, maiden, children, friend, lover—and that's the benefit I see in this fairy tale.

I don't know about you, but for the longest time I mistakenly believed that my life was a story about me. The routine I go through each and every day is *my* life. This being the case, I have a vested interest in how my life turns out. When I see the script take a turn I don't like—one that I perceive as unfair—I lobby for a change to the script, threaten a strike if I don't get what I want, and ultimately claim that I am entitled to a fair standard in my life.

But the story is not about me. It's about God. I play a supporting role. I can study my life and find a small story within the larger story, but if I want to glimpse my part in God's life, I must look to the larger story, support his lead, and play my part in the great story of God's redemption.

Life is not fair. And in the way we define fair, God is not fair. But I don't think we want God to be fair. If God were fair, we would all be in hell. No, life is about the part we play in God's amazing true fairy tale. Just as the fairy tales we read as children began, "Once upon a time," and concluded with the relieved sigh, "and they all lived happily ever after," so Genesis begins and Revelation ends.

I am fascinated by this question: What is the small role I play in the feature-length drama starring God? And that question begets a follow-up: Am I doing a convincing job playing my role?

All of the great saints lived lives that declared God worthy and trustworthy (see Heb. 11:35–40). They died believing—playing a convincing role—whether they could see the conclusion or not. They lived by faith. That is, they placed their confidence in God and the belief that he is honorable to the end and cannot lie.

The fact that Christ prevails in the end and defeats the great red dragon of Revelation is made more phenomenal by all those who went before him and whom the great dragon thought he had devoured in ignominy. By leaving their bones hanging in the briar forests of life, the devil warns all comers.

But the grizzly scene at the edge of the briar forest is part of the buildup to the end of the story. Who would guess that anyone would attempt to overcome such a curse just to rescue a lost and hopeless, sleeping race surrounded by thorns, a great dragon, and a foreboding castle?

Everyone, except for those who died attempting to hack their way through the briars and the one who was ultimately successful, lived their lives believing that what they saw around them was all the happiness they could hope for in life. They were satisfied with the telling of the legend of the sleeping princess. But the one who plays the lead in the tale has a different vision. He brings the legend to life and will not be satisfied until the story ends, "and they all lived happily ever after."

As for John, why should it matter how he was killed? His death was precious to God (see Ps. 116:15). His death delivered him from earth's dimension to heaven's. His death initiated his reception of the highest award a man will ever receive. John's death made it possible for God to tell him to his face, "Well done, son. You did a fine job and delivered a compelling performance." His death accomplished what his heart sought to accomplish: a way for the Messiah.

The fact that John died by beheading is of no more significance in the scheme of things than if he had died by heart attack or camel stampede. What is important is that he played his part to the end, setting the stage for the lead player to ultimately bring the story to its conclusion.

I cannot imagine that John is lingering over his wasted, shortened life or the despicable exit forced upon him by the godless. He is simply delighted to be living with the One who will finish for all time what he helped usher in by preparing the way. John's excitement today must be similar to that of the actors and actresses who play their part on stage and then gather to watch the premiere, see the finished product, and have dinner afterward.

Besides, had John died a true martyr's death, perhaps the pathway he prepared for the Messiah would have been jeopardized by leading his followers to see him as the subject of life. As it was, his death left nothing but disgust and disillusionment. These powerful incentives goaded mankind to long for and listen to Jesus' message of deliverance: "I am the way, and the truth, and the life; no one comes to the Father, but through Me" (John 14:6).

In his death, John was true to the purpose and calling God had for him. Even in death, he prepared the way of the Lord. Our lives, like John's, are not about what we possess or the comfort with which we live or die. We are part of something much larger than the small universe we call life. It is not possible for our small story to end with happiness ever after. This is a temporary place and an interim assignment.

As for me, I'm convicted that I still hold to a legalistic attitude, believing I can enhance my favor with God by what I do or don't do. And when languishing with this belief, I often find myself distracted with whether or not the temporal I consider permanent is fair or not. I'm convicted again that the feature story is not about me. It is about God. Like John, hopefully I'm pointing the way. I'm convicted of how easy it is to choose to live in the small story I've created, while missing the larger story God has plotted and cast. Once again, I'm reminded that he is the lead, and I the support, in the cast of characters. I believe John would be, or perhaps is, pleased that his death serves as this reminder to me. Interestingly, he is still pointing the way and preparing it.

Life, fundamentally and quite simply, is not about what I do, what I gain, who I know, or how I die. Life is about knowing Christ, walking with God, and allowing the Holy Spirit to guide me in fulfilling my role in the great tale of God come down to rescue a fallen, debauched people from the greatest evil the universe has ever known, while proposing a marriage of hearts, with the promise that we shall live happily ever after.

What others think of how my part plays out in this great tale is of secondary importance to my determination to play my part as a supporting actor in God's story. Should I be caught up to heaven and miss death, pass quietly in the night, fight an agonizing exit due to some dread disease, or lose my head for a foolish, drunken oath made during lustful revelry, so be it. The means by which I exit is largely beside the point and has little to do with my life, other than putting a period or exclamation point at the end of my sentence. My destiny is to develop the plot of this short, but very large, story of the main character's adventure to win his true love.

Further, I want to access what is due me from Father's kind hand and grace-filled heart in heaven, not here. My Fort Worth home is not heaven—though I think it's wonderful—nor are any of the extraordinary places I have visited or read about. And should I succumb to the temptation to set down roots in the places I see and am even inspired by, I will miss my important part in the large story of God and opt to act in the small story of my own creation.

Of course, having said all this, I must point out that what the larger story suggests is that I am the sleeping beauty. I am the noble cause behind the hero's courageous entry into the briar forest to have it out with the dread dragon. In addition to my role as a supporting actor, I am also the reason the story was begun.

The opening line of the story, "Once upon a time," casts me in the same place that the conclusion, "and they all lived happily ever after," does. It is only through writing my supporting part into the intermediate part of the story that I can begin to comprehend the person of Christ, his grace to me, and my importance to him.

I know the larger story concludes, "and they all lived happily ever after," and I know I will witness the end of the story one of these days. But while I read that God will wipe away all our tears and that there will be no sorrow and heartache in heaven, I am motivated now—while I am on the stage of life—to play my part well because I can't help but believe this will make my celebration after the performance sweeter.

Thus, there is hope for tomorrow, and determination for today, that when the curtain is drawn, and I consider the part I played and the way I performed it, I will have the ecstasy of saying, "Oh, wow!" and not the remorse of, "Oh, no!"

### Something to Consider

What part do you play in God's fairy tale?
What part have you been attempting to play?
Do you really want God to be fair with you?

No, me either. I think the whole question—accusation really—of whether God is fair or not comes from the dragon. His motive is to keep us from Father, undermine our trust, and isolate us from the great heart that would do anything to win our hearts.

I don't want to carry the parallel of the "Sleeping Beauty" fairy tale too far, but it does occur to me that when I attempt to live independently of Father, rather than rely upon Jesus to live life through me, my life takes on many of the characteristics I imagine must have existed around the silent castle in "Sleeping Beauty." There is little passion, little life, only measured beauty, and little diversity.

What's the story of your life? Is it a short story starring you, or is it part of a larger story, as John's life was?

## MEDITATION
### & RESPONSE

*Father, I don't want to live in my story as I conceive it. I want to live in your story. I want to be part of your vision, dream your dreams with you, and stay focused on the real ending to the story rather than what seems plausible.*

*It never would have occurred to me to put myself into the tale twice, once as a supporting actor and again as the heroine, so to speak. But if I didn't play both parts, I would never be able to appreciate your genius or the role you play.*

*You didn't have to do that, Father. You could have just used me up, sort of like an extra in the movies. Or you could have left me asleep the whole time while you performed your part. But you included me, shared the stage with me, and invited me to the premiere and celebratory banquet and ball afterwards.*

*I accept!*

*Thanks, Papa.*

# nineteen

# Darkness

As a kid I had yellow, footy pajamas that were faded to the color of a manila folder, but whoever handed them down to me did a good thing. Oh, to have another pair, size medium.

It was always a little tough getting the bottoms on after getting out of the bathtub, but when I was visiting my granddad in Poteau, Oklahoma, I could count on his help. It's not that he was so intent on helping me get my pajamas on, it's just that we couldn't sit down to our before-bed cornbread and milk until I was dressed for bed.

While Granddad, my brother Mason, and I sat at the formica-topped table and ate our bedtime snack, Mom got the bed ready. Mason slept like a West Texas windmill, and the only hope of a decent night's sleep was to roll a quilt up lengthways and put it down the middle of the bed under the covers. I can still feel that quilt up against my back as I snuggled against it. Mom would tuck the covers under the mattress, turn out the light, and close the door.

Granddad Hoyle lived on ten acres at the foot of "Granddaddy's Mountain"—you know, the one the bear went over to see what he could see. When the lights were turned out at Granddad's, I'm here to tell you, it got dark—so dark that I couldn't see my brother eighteen inches away or even my hand in front of my face. But through the darkness, on the other side of the door, I could hear Dad and Granddad talking.

In the summertime, when I'd ride the bus to Poteau by myself, the dark room was even darker, or so it seemed. Mason wasn't beside me, the quilt wasn't rolled up at my back, the covers weren't tightly tucked in, and I couldn't hear my granddad talking. But I knew he was there, just on the other side of the darkness. He'd told me so, and he'd never left me before.

Although the darkness tempted me to bail out of bed, Granddad's steel blue eyes had conveyed to me that in bed, in the dark, was the best place for me to be until morning. And besides, what evil could befall me?

Just moments earlier, sitting out in the side yard, Granddad told stories of scaring off catamounts (mountain lions), catching foxes in the hen house, and killing rattlesnakes under the carport. All was well. The only difference between the daylight of tomorrow and the darkness enveloping the bedroom was that I couldn't see. But that didn't alter the fact that I was secure.

As you know so well, darkness isn't limited to the front bedroom at Granddaddy's house. Life is full of dark times: When questions multiply like rabbits and answers are few and far between, emotions screech and anguish occupies the front row in your mind's theater. Such stress passes its effect to the body, and sleepless nights collaborate with oppressive days, gauntness replaces the sparkle that was in your eye, and frustration oozes out from under fraying edges.

To add to these dark places, it often seems as though God has gone on an extended trip to the outer sectors of the universe and is unavailable for comment. At a time when life is driving us deeper into darkness and our inclination is to cry out to the Lord more fervently, surely he should be more available.

Darkness seems to breed deeper darkness, and vulnerability to Satan's schemes is significantly heightened. The old adage, "When it rains, it pours," certainly seems to apply. And so you hunker down to wait out God's extended trip, try to resist the temptation to run, and wish for a sense of security in the darkness.

Perhaps the deepest, darkest book of the Bible is Job. Job mentions darkness over thirty times. That's over 40 percent of the Old Testament references to darkness, all contained in this one book. And you say, "I identify! You ought to read my journal. If I could bring myself to write a book, it would rival Job's." Like Job, while sitting in the midst of insidious, black, all-pervasive darkness, you too are calling out for a God that seemingly doesn't answer.

But is the reputation of darkness all that it's cracked up to be? Is darkness really that deep? Is it honestly the absence of light, especially the light of Christ? Are our only options to hunker down and wait for morning or cut and run in any direction, hoping to stumble upon a flicker of light somewhere in the dark?

What would you say if I told you that the opposite was in fact the truth about darkness? Have you ever noticed Isaiah 45:3? "I will give you the treasures of darkness and hidden wealth of secret places, so that you may know that it is I, the LORD, the God of Israel, who calls you by your name."

Did you catch the part about "treasures of darkness"? Or what about wealth that is hidden in secret places? And most importantly, did you see that the Lord is in the darkness, the hidden and secret places?

Oh, how often the enemy accuses Father of being out to lunch when we are in a spot and can't see our hand in front of our face. But such is not the case. Darkness holds fortunes of faith that the daylight can't reveal. Hidden and secret places harbor riches that aren't available to those clinging to the crown of their own sufficiency and walking the common course. And for all of Satan's ranting and raving, take special notice of the fact that God is in the dark place, calling you by name, identifying himself so that you won't be afraid.

I've never liked being called "son." Around our house, being called "son" was the rough equivalent to being called by both my first and middle names, and that only occurred when I was in trouble. However, there was one exception: Granddad. When I was visiting Grandmom and him, at bedtime he'd turn out the light, stand in the doorway, look back at me tucked securely into bed, and say, "Good night, son. Sleep good. We've got a big day tomorrow." And then he'd close the door. With hope for tomorrow and the voice of someone I trusted explicitly still echoing in my ears, I was enveloped in the dark.

If Satan is successful with his temptations, we'll view the darkness as a sign of God's disfavor, even abandonment, and think of the dark as an unpleasant and sinister place to be viewed with suspicion. Instead of seeing ourselves securely tucked within the covers of God's gracious care, we'll buy the enemy's lie and grope along the walls searching desperately and indignantly for a way of escape, oftentimes at any cost. Such behavior is unnecessary and is not indicative of people who are confident of Father's care.

David knew all about the darkness. In fact, many of the Psalms were penned during dark periods in his life—always on the move, hiding in caves, living in the wilderness, and running for his life. In Psalm 18:11 David talks about whom he found in those dark places. "He made dark-ness His secret place; His canopy around Him, darkness of waters, thick clouds of the skies."

How dense is the fog? How deep are the waters? How dark is it? The Lord inhabits those places. You may not be able to see and may be having difficulty keeping your head above the rising waters, but Father is in those places. He hides there waiting for you, not to scare you, but to share with you his treasures.

Relax. Step in under the canopy, even though it is dark and thick. He is there and has made the deep, dense fog his shelter. He invites you to join him.

Let me encourage you not to rush for answers. Take time to talk with Father in the sanctity of his canopy of darkness. Tell him what's on your mind, what your dilemmas are, and verbalize the questions you are struggling with. He may give you immediate input, but he may be silent, not because he is angry, but because he knows you have everything you need right that moment. Sometimes the best thing he can do is listen and reassure you simply by his presence.

Don't forget that Jesus asked for an answer when he prayed in the Garden and didn't get one; otherwise, he wouldn't have asked three times. But God was there, and Jesus knew it. He kept talking, and Father kept listening.

I mentioned Job earlier in this chapter. This man, so well acquainted with darkness, writes in his book, "He [God] reveals mysteries from the darkness and brings the deep darkness into light" (12:22). If I'm looking for answers to the deep questions I'm facing, most likely they will come from the darkness. And the deeper the darkness, the more I must focus on the fact that the Lord brings even the deep dark into light. In other words, I won't be in the dark forever. God will give me the treasures of the dark-ness, and they will be in such a form that I'll be able to see them one day in the light.

145

And speaking of light, Jesus says, "What I tell you in the darkness, speak in the light; and what you hear whispered in your ear, proclaim upon the housetops" (Matt. 10:27). You won't be in the dark forever, and when you do emerge, do as David did. Broadcast to all who will listen your testimony of his grace: "The Lord met me in my dark time." Endorse his work in your life. Emblazon your testimony with the fact of God's sufficiency and the light of Christ in your life.

Calm down and relax. Embrace the darkness and listen for the Lord. He is there and will use the darkness to invest treasures in your life that are inconceivable to you right now. And when the light dawns, you will indeed have something to shout about from the housetops.

"Wake up, boy; we've got a big day. Did you sleep good? Did you get cold?" It never crossed Granddad's mind to ask if it was too dark. It wasn't. He was there and had been all night.

## Something to Consider

I woke up the other night and was aware of Father's presence in the room. I began to pray, mostly by listening, but I asked, "Father, what's on your mind?" The impression that returned was astounding to me. "Nothing much. I just wanted to talk with you."

I think the panic that often overcomes us in the darkness is a desperate play by Satan to thwart what could be an intimate, profound moment with Father.

There are no distractions in the dark. Nothing to do but listen and talk. No horizon to pursue, only the moment. No stimulation but solitude. These are important moments to Father, and I intend to give them priority as well.

What are the dark places in your life right now? Have you ever thought about reframing them? Instead of deep, dark foreboding, have you considered they might be treasures?

## MEDITATION & RESPONSE

*Father, I can only assume that the darkness surrounding me has the potential to be a cache of spiritual treasure I have only dreamed about. I want to step in under the canopy of your grace in the dark density of my ungracious places. And not just to attempt to shorten the night of my discontent and pain. I want to be where you are and soak up everything you have for me of your grace and, in this case, your grace in a dark, ungracious place.*

*Would you turn my vision of the dark into your vision? Would you teach me to listen for your voice in my dark places? Would you ease my panic with a greater awareness of your presence?*

*As I have said before, Father, I want to go where you are going and do what you are interested in doing. Take me with you. A journey without you is only a trip, and I have been on enough of those already.*

*Thanks, Papa.*

# Grace in
# Insecure
# Places

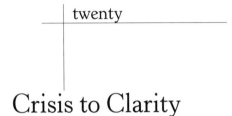

twenty

# Crisis to Clarity

When was the last time you told yourself you did a good job? For me it had been forty-three years. I have a special place where God speaks to me: the parking lot in back of the office, over by the dumpsters. I didn't choose this place, God did. And who am I to wonder about God's affinity with the back parking lot? Actually, I've concluded it isn't the lot, but the time I spend walking across it to buy a cup of coffee at the gas station on the corner.

One morning as I arrived at the office, I was greeted by a potentially significant problem. Our executive director was out of the office, so this firestorm was mine to fight and contain. Forty-five minutes later equilibrium was regained, and I was strolling across the back lot toward the gas station, thinking about the averted problem.

I realized as I walked that I had done a good job of dealing with the issues troubling the troops. But almost as soon as I was aware of having done a good job, I also thought of how I could have done the job better. As has been my custom for all but a few weeks of my life, I launched into a critical self-evaluation process to assess how to improve my performance as a leader the next time I am given an opportunity like the one just encountered.

But this morning, for the first time, I was cognizant of an awkward feeling associated with having done a good job, and it got my attention. *What is that about?* I wondered as I walked. *Why am I so uncomfortable with acknowledging that I did a good job?* Father was trying to get my attention.

For all of my determination to do a good job today and a better job tomorrow, I was missing the joy of the good today for the aspiration of doing better tomorrow. Of course, you know as well as I do, tomorrow never comes. As a result, today's success is never enjoyed. Consequently, I had never told myself, "Pres, you did a good job."

In my methodical manner, I was not satisfied with accepting this revelation at face value. After all, how could something this important happen by the dumpster? Instead, I asked the obvious question, out loud: "I wonder what the Bible has to say about this?"

Quick as a flash, Genesis 1 came to mind. That is of course the chapter that records God's creative genius in setting Earth spinning in its orbit, throwing the stars across the vault of heaven, and building boundaries for the seas. I was struck as I recalled what God said to himself with each stage of his creative work. "This is good."

The connect-the-dots puzzle in my mind was taking shape. Father is creating in me his characteristics. I am trusting him to guide me and direct me through his indwelling Spirit. If I truly believe this theology, then I must go where he is clearly taking me. I must side with him instead of my flesh, and now would be an appropriate time to begin.

And so, for the first time in forty-three years, I told myself I had done a good job. I stopped about twenty yards from the dumpsters and said audibly, "Pres, you did a good job of handling that situation in the office this morning."

Almost as if on cue, I heard the devil's temptation, disguised as my fleshly, condemning, parental voice. "Pres, if you go there—telling yourself you have done a good job—you will be slacking off in your commitment to be a godly man. Your life will soon be characterized by a slack hand and a series of compromises. You must not let this occur. My counsel is to return from this easy way. Adopt the strenuous course, the noble way, the high ground. Return to that high standard by which you have lived your life to date."

As is the case with any temptation from the enemy, there was a grain of truth in what he said. It is important for us to live a determined life, aspire to a noble standard, and refuse compromise. But while this is an important point, it was irrelevant to the issue at hand. Father was trying to tell me I had done a good job and get me to agree with him. After all, I had trusted him to guide me and express himself through me as I stepped into the middle of the office firestorm. As one warrior to another, he was simply celebrating after the battle by saying, "We did a good job, you and I."

Implied within that confident declaration is his conviction: "I will go with you into battle again." But perhaps more important, he wanted to walk across the parking lot with me right then. And he wanted to be sure I got the message for the moment: "Pres, you did a good job."

How long has it been since you told yourself, "Good job"? Well, neighbor, that's too long.

## Something to Consider

Acknowledging a job well done has been an amazing paradigm shift for me, not to mention a tremendous motivation. God's voice of encouragement is far more powerful than the enemy's recommendation that deeper examination and harder work for the future be the focus. It is as though a new horizon has appeared before me.

Once again, I am confronted with my old nemesis of legalistic thinking and living, served up on a golden platter by the devil: "If I can do better than I just did, sooner or later God is going to like me more than he does right now." At its core, legalism leads me to believe I can enhance my standing with God through the way I perform.

Is that true? Will God be more pleased with you if you perform differently? No. It is not possible to increase God's pleasure in you. Make no mistake about it, God will encourage you to correct your course occasionally so your performance more accurately reflects who you are, but this has nothing to do with gaining God's favor. Father accepts you if you are in Christ. Period.

This fact has set me free to perform without all the pressure of legalism. And it has opened the way for me to celebrate my successes, be more candid about my failures, and listen without threat to the constructive criticism I receive.

I am secure in Christ. I know I am okay in Father's eyes. That is very different from constantly trying to enhance my performance in an effort to become okay with God. From my perspective, this grace has set me free from the ungraciousness of an impossible standard.

## MEDITATION & RESPONSE

*Father, I appreciate your encouragement
and affirmation. Thank you for not letting me
off on the point of telling myself the truth
about the good job I did.*

*It occurs to me, Papa, that I did a good job
on two things. I did a good job with the mess at
the office, and I did a good job of trusting you
as well. And what is especially interesting is
that the mess at the office could have degener-
ated into a major catastrophe, but if I trusted
you—which I did—then you would have
affirmed me for the good job I did of depending
upon you even if the results didn't look right.*

*I want to trust you, and I want to bring
honor to you and your kingdom. But I do feel
ungracious pressure to perform. Help me see
that this pressure comes from the enemy and
not from you. I want my perspective to be
rooted in your perspective.*

*And Father, help me celebrate my victories.
Thanks, Papa.*

# twenty-one

# Insignificance
# to Contentment

I read Jesus' Sermon on the Mount in *The Message* recently and was struck by Eugene Peterson's translation of Matthew 5:5: "You're blessed when you're content with just who you are—no more, no less."

The first thought that came to mind was another passage of Scripture, "You shall love your neighbor as you love yourself" (Matt. 22:39). Perhaps the most elementary point of this verse is that if I don't love myself, and I am not content with who I am, my neighbor isn't going to be very appreciative of my attempts at loving him.

I can assent to loving myself, but the proof of my love will be in my contentment with Pres. As I thought about it, I realized I had a nice, neat, theological perspective of myself. I am accepted, loved, forgiven, sanctified, justified, seated with Christ in heavenly places.

But after reading Peterson's translation and pondering the idea of being content with who I am, I returned to Father with a follow-up question concerning my identity in Christ. "Father, I readily agree with you about my identity in Christ and in your family and I am deeply appreciative, but the characteristics describing me are the same characteristics describing everyone in your family. Papa, who am I? Who is Preston Gillham in your eyes? How can I be content with who I am if I'm uncertain about my unique identity as an individual?"

I grew quiet and began to listen to the thoughts that streamed into my mind, and I believed by faith that the thoughts were from Father. Perhaps what was most astounding, even though it was right before my eyes all along, was the way Father had woven his identity through the characteristics of my personality. I agreed with Scripture, stating that Christ is my life, but I captured some portion of what contentment is as I listened to Father describe me.

And then there was the finale from Father: *Pres, the jealousy, bitterness, resentment, discontent, and entitlement you fight against are indicative of your failure to be content with who you are. You are attempting to gain contentment rather than being content. Stop striving and driving and pushing to prove yourself. Relax in who I have made you to be, no more, no less. It is only then that you will be content.*

I guess you pretty well know what I'm trusting Christ for right now in my life after reading that. Not only do I want to be free of the ungracious struggles that hound me, but I want to love others as a genuine demonstration of God's love to them. But there is another aspect of this verse that motivates me. When the Scripture says, "Love others like you love yourself," it occurs to me that one of the others I'm supposed to love as I love myself is God.

What an amazing individual Father is. For much of my life I desperately sought to gain God's love. It didn't occur to me that God wanted my love—the kind I give to myself—much less that he could be satisfied with the love I gave him.

He is always working the relationship angle, isn't he? His logic in this arena seems cyclical as I consider it. "For whoever wishes to save his life will lose it; but whoever loses his life for My sake will find it," he says (Matt. 16:25). He lays down his life so I can live. I lay down my life, and he lives in another, who lays his life down, and the body of Christ is perpetuated and God's kingdom enriched.

By being content with who I am, I become content with who he is. By being content with who he is, I become content with who I am. By being content with him and with myself I convey contentment to others—and the cycle of life in Christ continues to be demonstrated through the manifestation of his grace.

How about you? Are you content with who you are? Or more fundamentally, have you asked Father to help you understand who *you* are?

### Something to Consider

I want to ask you to consider two things that are highlighted in the paragraphs you have just read. First, consider your identity in Christ. He says some outrageous things about you in his Book.

Many of us have clung to the self-image the world has given us. Others of us cling to the self-image religion has espoused about us—sinner, worm, despicable, failure—and we even have Bible verses to document this belief. But in truth, what others think and what religion says must be weighed against what Father says, not vice versa. We will never arrive at the self-image Father has in mind for us if we start backwards and begin with what others say. What does Father say about you in his Word?

Second, God details dozens of our amazing characteristics throughout his Word. But we also have a driving need to find our place of uniqueness in the world. Would you consider praying the prayer I prayed: "Father, I know who I am in the body of Christ, but who am I as an individual?"

Each year my brothers and I go on a fly-fishing trip. Without fail, the wait staff at the restaurant or the clerks at the hotel will look at the three of us lined up and say, "Wow! Nobody could doubt that you are brothers." But while the three of us look a lot alike, we are very much individuals.

As a believer, a Christian, a member of the body of Christ, and a resident of God's kingdom, you are accepted, holy, blameless, justified, sanctified, redeemed, and a participant in God's triumphal procession. You, like me and the other members of the family, share these characteristics and personhood in Christ, and you must come to agree with Father about these characteristics before you move on to answering the second question: What distinguishes you from all the other believers in the family of God?

I encourage you to do as I did: Get quiet and listen for Father's recounting of this to you. It will be a blessing to hear what Father thinks of you and to see yourself as he sees you—the unique, the one and only, you!

## MEDITATION
### & RESPONSE

*Father, this is a supreme challenge. I am having a hard enough time believing what you* say about me in your Scriptures, let alone contemplating my personal identity.

But I know this is important. I memorized the verse about loving you and loving others as I love myself years ago, and since those Sunday school days, I have quoted it often. Now here I am, much older, and the verse I learned as a child has turned my world upside down with its profound power. To think your satisfaction will be enhanced by my loving you. Father, only you would try this on me!

And I see your point. I must reassess who I am and redefine how to love myself for I have been ruthless with me. It would be inexcusable to try loving you as I have loved myself. And it is unreasonable to think others will be drawn to you if I love them as I have loved myself.

Thank you that who I am, how loved I am, and how I love others is based upon your standard instead of the standards I have labored under. There is no doubt about it, I live in an ungracious place, and I have behaved ungraciously toward myself. Father, in your still, small, unobtrusive but methodical way, your grace screams to me of your determination to love me. Your heart has won my allegiance. Thank you for pursuing me, staying on my trail, and not letting me out of your sight or your care. Your grace is compelling.

*I see your plan: As I exemplify your life and live a life representative of your grace, others will be drawn to share in the incredible bond we enjoy. I want to facilitate that desire of your heart. I want to extend your grace through the way I live life, carry myself, and speak of you, so that others might catch a glimpse of you. I want to be an advocate on your behalf, Father.*

*You have given me grace to live in the ungracious places of my world. But Father, would you grant me the grace to enter others' places of un-grace, demonstrate your love to them, reflect your heart by sharing my own, and lead them to your life by laying down my own?*

*Thanks, Papa.*

twenty-two

# Apathy to Contribution

A s a kid I was enthralled by Teddy Roosevelt's biog-
raphy. After he had ridden with the Rough Riders
up San Juan Hill and returned to the United States
a hero, he delivered one of his most famous speeches: "If
we are to be a really great people, we must strive in good
faith to play a great part in the world. We cannot avoid
meeting great issues. All that we can determine for ourselves is whether we shall meet them well or ill."

There is a healthy balance in TR's words. Greatness is
not hampered by difficult circumstances or tough issues.
In fact, greatness would not be great unless there were
monumental challenges to overcome. Victory would not
be sweetly savored unless defeat had been stared in the eye.

Meeting challenges is inevitable. Jesus said so when he told the disciples, "In the world you have tribulation" (John 16:33). But rather than launch into a discussion of how we are to deal with personal burdens, I would like for us to consider one of the great issues in our private lives.

Although TR wasn't talking about Christianity in his Chicago speech, his words apply. "If we are to be a really great people, we must strive in good faith to play a great part in the world." Our individual relationship with Christ is intensely personal on the one hand; but on the other, we are to be beacons of light to those around us. We are to actively intervene on people's behalf against the enemy as he tries his best to railroad them into his program. We are to be beacons of Father's grace in ungracious places.

All around us there are people struggling with various challenges. For some it's a self-image problem, while for others it's a closet full of masks and skeletons. Whether fronts, facades, or walls, competence, acceptance, or self-worth, it makes no difference what the fleshly tactic is; anything of the flesh is sin, and ultimately the consequences will demand their due.

What greater issue is there than to understand the magnitude of what God did in Christ at the cross? What more appropriate place is there for grace than in the home turf of un-grace? As TR said, "We cannot avoid meeting great issues," and this is an issue that affects all of us, and it is the greatest issue in all of history. While much of life is nondescript and bland, such is not the case in the spiritual realm of the heart. Paul writes, "For the flesh sets its desire against the Spirit, and the Spirit against the flesh; for these are in opposition to one another" (Gal. 5:17a). When grace and un-grace meet, the encounter is not peaceable but passionate. Grace flourishes in ungracious places (Rom. 5:20). As people of grace bonded to our Father at the heart, we are meant to meet the great issue of un-grace in ungracious places in the confidence of grace. If we consistently intervene in the lives of our family, friends, colleagues, and associates with a life exemplifying Christ's grace, and if we tactfully seize the opportunity to verbally reinforce this to them, we address this greatest of all issues and affect the world in a great way.

What greater contribution can we make to the world than to disciple believers and unbelievers in their understanding of all that Christ accomplished? In addition, there are many who have known Christ for years but not fully comprehended all that God did in Christ at the cross. Being saved from sin will do the believer little earthly good if he doesn't understand who he is and who Christ is in him.

Jesus Christ is the demonstration of God's determination to share his heart with us. It is Christ's life—the physical demonstration of grace—that the Holy Spirit desires to reproduce in and through us. We must choose to let the Spirit shine through our lives.

We can buy the enemy's lie and try to cast off this great issue of life as nonessential. But the best thing to do is to determine to trust Christ as we meet this issue head-on and allow the Spirit of Christ to express his life to others through us.

Grace in ungracious places: We have seen the pattern as we have read together. First, Father works diligently to share his heart with us. Second, Father waits for our response to his grace. And third, he trains us in the security and profundity of his grace as we reconcile the ungracious places in which we find ourselves with his always-abounding grace.

Does this call for us to boldly confront anyone and everyone with the reality of Christ's work? For some this is reasonable. But for most of us, we are to demonstrate Father's grace with a lifestyle that consistently reflects Christ's life. On a few occasions, we might have to say a word or two!

**Something to Consider**

All of us have personal challenges and hurdles, but confronting others with the life-changing message of Christ's finished work at the cross is indeed a great mission. You are on the front lines of this battle as you unfold each day at home, work, school, and in the world's forums. You play a great part in influencing your world through the life you live.

There are those who believe sharing your faith requires you to knock on doors, confront people on elevators, and corner seatmates on airplanes. For some this is appropriate, but for most it is not. If you are in passionate pursuit of Father, seizing every opportunity to grasp the magnitude of his grace and integrate it into your being, your life will scream a witness for the certitude of God and the compulsion of his invitation through the ages: "All may come!"

How do you know if you are being timid in sharing your faith? How do you know if you are one of the folks who should be engaging people with the gospel of Christ early on in your relationship with them?

If, in the other arenas of your life, you conduct yourself in an aggressive, enthusiastic manner, then you will find an aggressive assault up your San Juan Hill to be natural. On the other hand, if you move more slowly in relationships, building bonds with people a brick at a time, then your approach will be more measured and opportunistic. Advancing the great issue of grace in ungracious places will most likely have approximately the same feel for you as approaching the other important matters in your life.

Is this an absolute rule? No, not at all. Father often asks us to step outside the box of our lives and see his sufficiency from a different angle. His assumption is he doesn't like living in a box and you are his offspring, so why should you want to live in a box? You know enough of grace to know you are safe in Father's hands. You are secure.

In addition, you know how to listen to Father, to be quiet in the dark times, the silent times, and the uncertain times. I encourage you to pay attention and listen for Father's voice. He will call your name, and your heart will desire to respond. Do so! Follow his lead. There is no place so ungracious, no distance so great, no sin so profound, and no darkness so dark that his grace will not abound.

Where are the ungracious places Father desires to advance his grace through you?

# Meditation
## & Response

*Father, I give you my heart. Please help me comprehend the inseparable bond between us. I give you my soul. Please use me as your representative. I give you my life. Please help it reflect our relationship.*

*But Father, I also give you the ungracious places in my world. I need to see your grace instead of casting my own vision and interpretation of these circumstances. Please fill me with the awareness of your joy and contentment. I know you have already blessed me with these things, but my senses need to be sharpened to grasp them.*

*And Father, more than anything, please guide me into your confidence. I have no interest in perpetuating my own story in place of*

167

*yours. I want the assurance that the course I'm taking is your course, the story I'm living is your story, and the security I'm feeling is your confidence. Please, don't let me be satisfied with anything less. I have no desire to fall short of your grace.*

*Thanks, Papa.*

# twenty-three

# Insecurity to Confidence

A friend of mine says the worst sins are the ones we do not commit. The enemy of our souls will try any angle, won't he? Even suggesting a judgment of sin based upon perceived value. The fact is, sin is sin. Certainly different sins have different consequences, but sin has no value. Comparing your sins with another's to feel better about your failures is ungracious thinking, misses the point of grace, and demonstrates a lack of spiritual confidence.

While sin has no value, the people who commit sin— that would be you and me—have inestimable worth. I am convinced Christ went to hell to find us, offer redemption for us, and extend grace to us. The ghastliness of our sins

pales when compared to the atrocity of hell. Yet Jesus—
the personification of grace—went into that place of
absolute un-grace in order to offer us abounding grace
even at our greatest point of need.

One of the fundamental truths of Scripture is that
Christ gave his life for us so he could give his life to us and
live his life through us. Given this, to what ungracious
place will he not go in order to demonstrate his grace?
What sin is worse than hell? What sin of un-grace is so
profound that he is intimidated by its vileness? At what
point does failure become fatal to the one who is life?
When does the shriek of war's un-grace create panic in
the Great Warrior? When does the despicableness of sin
become so repulsive that God determines it could not pos-
sibly merit Calvary's redemption? When does the wicked-
ness of sin stain more deeply than the ability of Christ's
blood to cleanse? When does the onus of sin outweigh the
worth of the person for whom Christ laid down his life?
When do we conclude that Christ's descent into hell, with
our curse on his head, was an insufficient sacrifice to give
birth to the redemption of grace?

We must never give assent to any of these claims. But
we often do by discounting the person wallowing in an
ungracious place because of sin. We often do when we
empower un-grace with value by demanding that it morph
into some semblance of grace before we will respond to
the laboring person as an extension of God's grace. We
often discount grace's abundant confidence by quarantin-
ing it from the ungraciousness of life. And what is worse,
we often perpetuate ungraciousness by calling our quali-
fied granting of grace's riches an accurate representation
of the life of Christ.

God will not be insulated, isolated, separated, quali-
fied, or quarantined from the ones he died to redeem. If
the un-grace of hell was insufficient to repulse him, if the
pain of Calvary was insufficient to cause him to have sec-

ond thoughts, then the ungraciousness of life will not slow him down in demonstrating his heart to us. Why should we do less?

Just as Jesus Christ lived in the world while maintaining his holiness, so he exhorts us to be in the world but not of it (ref. John 17). Right before he ascended, Jesus told us, "you shall be My witnesses" (Acts 1:8). This verse is often associated with salvation, and rightly so, but we qualify it by limiting where we will go to extend grace. Like the Pharisees, we place values on sin and assume that we are in less need of grace than the poor soul who is addicted to pornography. Or, like the woman at the well, we grant value to sin and assume our sin is too great to be overcome by the extravagance of grace.

Sin has no value. Only people toiling with the ungraciousness of sin have worth, and their worth is significant enough in God's mind to warrant the lavish abundance of grace. There will never be enough darkness to dispel the light, and according to Jesus we are the light of the world (Matt. 5:14).

Jesus Christ is grace in your ungracious place, and you are his advocate of grace in someone else's ungracious place. But not if you wallow in the pitiful insecurity of what effect someone else's sin might have on your reputation if you step into the un-grace of their world to demonstrate Christ's life.

We have been blessed with every spiritual blessing in the heavenly places, granted seats at the right hand of God, issued a heavenly passport, declared righteous, holy, blameless, and accepted through the finished work of Jesus Christ. We have been filled with the Holy Spirit, given a new heart, justified before a holy God, and cut from the spiritual fabric of his divine nature. Capitalizing on these declarations, in glorious prose sufficient to inspire even the most timid among us, Paul says:

What then shall we say to these things? If God is for us, who is against us? He who did not spare His own Son, but delivered Him over for us all, how will He not also with Him freely give us all things? Who will bring a charge against God's elect? God is the one who justifies; who is the one who condemns? Christ Jesus is He who died, yes, rather who was raised, who is at the right hand of God, who also intercedes for us. Who will separate us from the love of Christ? Will tribulation, or distress, or persecution, or famine, or nakedness, or peril, or sword? . . . But in all these things we overwhelmingly conquer through Him who loved us. For I am convinced that neither death, nor life, nor angels, nor principalities, nor things present, nor things to come, nor powers, nor height, nor depth, nor any other created thing, will be able to separate us from the love of God, which is in Christ Jesus our Lord.

Romans 8:31–35, 37–39

Take special note of the last sentence in this passage: There is nothing that possesses the power to separate us from our heritage. Father will not hear of it. If he went to hell to get us, how likely is he to lose his hold on us?

You are secure! You are as secure as Father's hand is big. You are as secure as he is strong. You are as secure as he is bound by his integrity. You are as secure as God's promise to be faithful. You are as secure as Father's love demonstrated in Christ. You are as secure as his life is eternal. You are as secure as Christ's provision for sin is sufficient. You are as secure as Jesus' promises. You are as secure as God is divine by nature. You are as secure as God's love for you. You are as secure as Father's grace is abundant. You are secure!

So walk confidently as a manifestation of God's grace. Take up his confidence as yours and demonstrate grace. In the confidence of his grace, live a life of grace. With the confidence that Christ is in you to express his life through you, extend grace. In the confidence that you are a recipient of grace, unfurl your life in the storms of ungraciousness and demonstrate God's grace.

With the confidence granted to you in Christ Jesus, substantiate grace by showcasing it in the ungracious places of life. Can you do this? Absolutely. Will you get the dirt of the world under your fingernails? Yes. Will you feel the stress of the un-grace around you? Yes, you will. Will some in the community of faith reject you for reaching into the world's arenas with grace? Sadly, they will. What should you do about that? See another opportunity to demonstrate grace in an ungracious place. Do not be mistaken; some of the most ungracious places in our lives are pews, fellowship halls, Sunday school rooms, pulpits, and seminaries. Do not be put off. Grace flourishes in ungracious places.

Grace: Demonstrate it. Share it. Live it. Let yourself be caught up in it. Be astonished by it. Marvel at it. Take it into your soul and treasure it. Give it safe harbor in your heart. Fix your eyes on it. Set your mind upon it. Take hold of it and adopt it. Love it. Respond to it. Cherish it. March to its beat. Dance to its tune. Rally to its cry. Join in its shout. Advance upon its signal. Lock arms with it. Depend upon it. Find your security in it. Place your confidence in it. Let its extravagance exude from the pores of your smile, the gleam in your eye, and the warmth of your touch.

But don't ever forget that grace is a person. Grace is his divine influence upon your heart. Grace is his fingerprint on your life. Grace is the determined demonstration of his heart. Grace is the bond between you and Father. Grace is the determination of a Father who is not afraid to get his hands dirty.

He sought you in your ungracious places and seeks you in the ungraciousness of your messes. He gives you the confidence to be his representative in the ungracious places around you. And he gives you the inspiration to be his representative simply through the security of your confidence in him. For "where sin increased, grace abounded all the more" (Rom. 5:20).

Grace is a divine heart, discontent to be by itself. Grace is God's determined effort to share his heart with us in hopes that we will see and recognize and acknowledge his overture, and say, "Oh, wow!"

## Something to Consider

Have you considered that the magnitude of grace is significant enough that you can leave the cloister of your presuppositions, prejudices, and plans and consider the fresh parameters Father wishes to show you?

Have you considered that you do not have to be careful with grace—as if it is a precipice from which you are going to fall?

Have you considered that grace is not a poor, pitiful acceptance of your destitution and victimization by the world? In other words, grace is not divine welfare or a spiritual social service.

Have you considered that grace cannot be exhausted, depleted, or reduced?

Have you considered that grace is God's desire? His manifestation? His persona? His advent? His incarnation?

Have you considered that grace is extravagant, lavish, outrageous, wild, and imprudent, and only becomes more so as the un-grace around you proliferates?

Have you considered what it will take for you to live a life of grace, and have you considered what that life will look like?

What will it take for you to summon the confidence and courage necessary to not only receive grace in your ungracious places, but to extend grace to others in their ungracious places?

Jesus put a face on grace.

## MEDITATION
### & RESPONSE

*Oh, wow!*
*Father, I understand better now.*
*Thanks, Papa.*
*Amen.*

**Preston Gillham** is the president and chairman of Lifetime Guarantee, Inc., a non-denominational Christian ministry located in Fort Worth, Texas. In addition to his work as an author, Pres speaks nationally and internationally to churches, conferences, and leadership organizations advocating a return to the standard of grace, the confidence of a right relationship with Jesus Christ, and the integration of these essentials into every aspect of life, leadership, and family.

Pres is the voice of "Everyday Grace," a short-feature radio program. He serves on several boards, is a content advisor for *New Man* magazine, and has consulted with a variety of non-profit organizations.

He is married to Dianne, who is a first-grade teacher, and is master—most of the time—to Honey, his barkless dog, who is a Basenji. He is an avid bicycle rider, motorcyclist, fly fisherman, and outdoorsman.

To find out more about Pres, additional materials, or to inquire about scheduling him for a speaking engagement, please call toll free, 888-395-LIFE (5433), or visit online at www.lifetime.org.